MW00565360

EFFECTIVE LEGAL WRITING

A GUIDE FOR STUDENTS AND PRACTITIONERS

Second Edition

■ ■ ■

Douglas E. Abrams
Associate Professor Emeritus of Law
University of Missouri School of Law

WEST
ACADEMIC
PUBLISHING

© 2016 LEG, Inc. d/b/a West Academic
© 2021 LEG, Inc. d/b/a West Academic
    444 Cedar Street, Suite 700
    St. Paul, MN 55101
    1-877-888-1330

West, West Academic Publishing, and West Academic are trademarks of West Publishing Corporation, used under license.

Printed in the United States of America

ISBN: 978-1-64708-745-6

To my law students past and present,
who continue to make me proud
that I am one of their teachers

ACKNOWLEDGMENTS

This book expands and refashions articles that I have written regularly for the past several years in The Missouri Bar's quarterly magazine and in the *Journal of the Missouri Bar*. I thank The Missouri Bar for letting me share perspectives about effective legal writing for so long. I also thank the Bar for permitting other states to republish several of the articles in their own bar journals. Most important, I thank The Missouri Bar for its constructive initiatives that advance the administration of justice.

Writing a book resembles playing sports because the outcome turns on teamwork. No player can win a game alone, and no author can write a book alone. I thank four all-stars for generously reviewing, editing, and improving these pages:

One all-star is my colleague, Professor Melody R. Daily, director emerita of our legal research and writing program at the University of Missouri School of Law. As director and as a veteran research and writing teacher who set the right example, Melody assembled talented colleagues who share her devotion for preparing students for law practice.

Professor Michael J. Lane, one of my 1L legal research and writing students in 1982–83, has been a successful New York City commercial litigation partner for three decades. As an adjunct professor of Legal Research and Writing at Fordham Law School since 1993, Mike holds his students' respect for sharing realism and practical insights.

Gary Toohey is a skilled writer who served as editor of the *Journal of the Missouri Bar* until his retirement at the end of 2020. Under his stewardship since 1984, the *Journal* maintained its deserved reputation for excellence.

Professor Dennis D. Crouch, is a talented teacher and writer, Co-Director of the University of Missouri School of Law's Center for Intellectual Property & Entrepreneurship, and editor of the popular patent law weblog, Patently-O.

* * *

Thank you also to deans Timothy J. Heinsz, R. Lawrence Dessem, Gary Myers, and Lyrissa Lidsky, whose leadership makes the University of Missouri School of Law such a vibrant place to teach and learn. Thank you to my colleagues Bob Bailey, Rafael Gely, and Joe Swanegan for their support as I wrote this Second Edition. And thank you to Kristen L.

Stallion, an excellent Missouri student and now alumna, for her outstanding editorial contributions.

DOUGLAS E. ABRAMS

March 1, 2021

SUMMARY OF CONTENTS

———

TABLE OF CONTENTS

PART 6. VERSATILITY

TABLE OF CASES

EFFECTIVE LEGAL WRITING

A GUIDE FOR STUDENTS AND PRACTITIONERS

Second Edition

PART 1

STARTING OUT

■ ■ ■

Lawyers do not practice the profession in Blackacre or some other mythical jurisdiction known only to law school classroom hypotheticals. As counselors and advocates in the private and public sectors, we spend careers practicing in the real world. We represent clients, and we advance causes. We appear before courts and administrators. We draft laws for legislators and rules and regulations for agencies. Versatile lawyers write about legal and non-legal issues in such diverse forums as newspapers, magazines, law reviews, state and local bar journals, and blogs.

Dean William L. Prosser called law "one of the principal literary professions" because "the average lawyer in the course of a lifetime does more writing than a novelist."[1] As a member of our law school's admissions committee for several years, I read a few thousand applications, including applicants' personal essays about why they seek careers in law. Many applicants say that they "want to help people and improve society." Applicants also view an honorable legal career as a source of personal fulfillment and professional respect. Soon after arriving for orientation, however, incoming 1Ls learn that achieving these aspirations, and almost any others in law, depends not only on a lawyer's values, ambitions, and fidelity to professional responsibility, but also heavily on the lawyer's writing ability.

This book concerns challenges and opportunities. In this first Part, Chapter 1 surveys criticisms of lawyers' writing and explores the central roles that writing skills play in the law school curriculum during and after the 1L year. Chapter 2 presents 12 basic strategies for achieving effective legal writing. The book's later Parts concern researching, writing, editing, dismantling barriers that impede effective written expression, and writing by versatile lawyers in one or more of the diverse forums recited at the end of the first paragraph above.

---

[1]   William L. Prosser, *English As She Is Wrote*, 7 J. Legal Educ. 155, 156 (1954–1955).

CHAPTER 1

"WE ARE ALL APPRENTICES"

. . .

Excellence in writing remains a lawyer's career-long pursuit. "We are all apprentices in a craft where no one ever becomes a master," novelist Ernest Hemingway said about writers.[1] If a lifetime writing apprenticeship was good enough for Nobel Laureate Hemingway, it is good enough for lawyers.

One eminent writer proud of his own lifetime apprenticeship was Hemingway's favorite sportswriter, Pulitzer Prize winner Red Smith, whose syndicated columns appeared several times each week in the *New York Herald Tribune* and other prominent newspapers nationwide for more than 45 years. Historian Daniel Okrent finds Smith "tall enough to stand shoulder-to-shoulder with the finest prose artists in twentieth-century American literature."[2] Two leading sportswriters praised Smith's columns for their unmatched "elegance and grace and precision . . . , each a gem of language."[3] Pulitzer Prize-winning journalist and historian David Halberstam, who produced lustrous gems himself, praised Smith's "deftly crafted" writing that "if anything got better over the years."[4]

The prolific Smith's quest for personal betterment reflected a lifetime of sustained hard work. When he began writing for the *New York Times* in 1971 near the twilight of his storied career, Smith remained dissatisfied with his work product. At 66, an age when people who are still working contemplate retirement, Smith assured the *Times* that he still considered himself an apprentice, seeking to "become simpler, straighter, and purer in my language."[5]

"Writing well," he explained, "always has been and always will be one of the most difficult of human endeavors. And it never gets easier."[6]

"TOO MUCH HEREINBEFORE PROVIDED WHEREAS"

Apprentices sometimes improve their skills through experience, but apprenticeship offers no guarantees. An imposing array of critics has long ridiculed lawyers' writing. In *Gulliver's Travels*, for example, Jonathan Swift complained that lawyers use "a peculiar cant and jargon of their own that no other mortal can understand."[7] In *Bleak House*, Charles Dickens derided lawyers' "liking for the legal repetitions and prolixities."[8] Through a protagonist, novelist Henry Fielding said that "nothing is more hurtful to a perfect knowledge of the law than reading it."[9]

Three-time Pulitzer Prize winner Carl Sandburg graces American literature as a poet, historian, novelist, and prominent biographer of lawyer Abraham Lincoln, the most elegant writer ever to occupy the White House. The *Boston Globe* said that Sandburg's writings "erupt into beauty and surge with power."[10] One author said that "[f]ew writers have been more popular in their time than" Sandburg.[11] The President's unmatched rhetoric may have helped attract biographer to subject.

Sandburg held a dim view of irksome legalese. In his poem, *The Lawyers Know Too Much*, he chided lawyers' writing for "Too many slippery ifs and buts and howevers,/ Too much hereinbefore provided whereas,/ Too many doors to go in and out of."[12]

"DULL QUALIFICATIONS AND CIRCUMLOCUTIONS"

Lawyers have long acknowledged their critics' point. In 1817, for example, Thomas Jefferson criticized his fellow lawyers for "making every other word a 'said' or 'aforesaid' and saying everything over two or three times, so that nobody but we of the craft can untwist the diction and find out what it means."[13]

As a Harvard law professor in 1931, Felix Frankfurter assailed "the inevitable lawyer's writing—the dull qualifications and circumlocutions that sink any literary barque or even freighter, the lifeless tags and rags that preclude grace and stifle spontaneity."[14] Five years later, Yale law professor Fred Rodell found "two things wrong with almost all legal writing. One is its style. The other is its content."[15]

"Lawyers' language," said a prominent New York attorney in 1954, "has long been regarded as the prime example of complex, unreadable, often unintelligible English."[16] In the 21st century, U.S. Circuit Judge Richard A. Posner finds it still "remarkable how badly the modern law student, modern law clerk, modern lawyer, and modern judge write."[17]

The lay public shares the frustration. After all these years, we still hear people say that so-and-so "writes like a lawyer." How often do we hear it meant as a compliment?[18] As professionals charged with safeguarding rights and obligations, lawyers owe it to their clients to overcome the heritage of public disdain, and to strive for more graceful, articulate written expression.

THE MOST IMPORTANT 1L COURSE

With experience and careful attention, law students and lawyers can hone written grace and articulateness over time. Writing apprenticeships ideally begin during elementary, secondary, and undergraduate education. But whether or not these early classroom years approach the ideal, law schools today typically offer writing requirements and opportunities taught by specialist professors who help prepare students for the challenges of law practice.

These requirements and opportunities did not always hold the place they warrant in the law school curriculum. In 1937, Professor Frankfurter wrote that "to turn out finished practising lawyers is not . . . the business of a university. . . . A law school is not a law office nor a court room."[19] Frankfurter's portrait left little room for general academic training in legal writing. In 1948, in the first issue of the *Journal of Legal Education*, University of Chicago law professor Harry Kalven Jr. confirmed that "law schools for the most part have signally failed to afford the law student opportunity for sustained exposition, other than the writing of examinations."[20]

In recent years, law school training in writing and other practical skills has gathered momentum as tuitions rise and the employment market for recent law graduates grows more challenging. The emphasis on skills-based legal education, which seemed novel until recently, has gone mainstream to help meet the needs and expectations of prospective law school applicants, and of enrolled law students who will soon enter the practice.

At all accredited law schools, writing experience begins with the first-year Legal Research and Writing requirement. For more than 30 years, I have told incoming students that this is their most important 1L course because it supplies the arsenal for ascertaining and applying doctrine and policy throughout their careers.

In law schools today, experiential learning typically extends not only to traditional first-year and upper-class doctrinal courses that sometimes integrate writing skills,[21] but also to upper-class skills-based courses, including electives in advanced legal research and writing. Writing opportunities mark participation on a law school's primary law review, specialty law reviews, and intramural and inter-school moot court teams. Writing experience also typically accompanies clinics, externships, and part-time student employment in the private and public sectors.

Both for present academic stimulation and future professional development, law students would be wise to pursue intensive writing throughout their studies. Until relatively recently, many larger firms helped develop their young associates' skills with in-house training seminars, including ones devoted to writing instruction and critique.[22] The firm's older lawyers might mentor the younger ones and help develop their expressive skills. Clients recognized that the work product of many young associates was not worth the steep hourly rates that some firms often charged for their work, but most institutional clients tolerated the discrepancy as a cost of doing business.

Clients today, however, increasingly balk at paying stiff legal fees for what they perceive as overpriced on-the-job training of newly minted associates.[23] Law firms and other legal employers sensing competitive pressures are left to parse applicants' transcripts, resumes, and writing samples for evidence of proficiency before day one in the office. Legal employers may grow impatient with recent hires whose writing falls short.[24]

The challenging employment market also leads some law graduates to open solo practices shortly after bar passage. Young solos rely more than ever on their law school writing experience because they miss out on in-house seminars, mentoring relationships, and similar professional buffers that once helped ease many newcomers into the profession.

"THE GREAT INVENTION OF THE WORLD"

"Writing—the art of communicating thoughts to the mind, through the eye—is the great invention of the world," said Abraham Lincoln in 1859, shortly before he left the Midwest for a wider stage.[25] Effective writing, explains novelist Stephen King, depends on sustained experience. "As with all other aspects of the narrative art," says King, "you will improve with practice, but practice will never make you perfect. Why should it? What fun would that be?"[26]

---

[1]   Robert Schmuhl, *Process vs. Product: For Some, the Act of Writing Can Be as Important as the Finished Work*, Chi. Trib., Apr. 2, 2000, at 14.3 (quoting Hemingway, N.Y. J.-Am., July 11, 1961).

[2]   Daniel Okrent, *Introduction*, in American Pastimes: The Very Best of Red Smith xix (Daniel Okrent ed., 2013); *see also* Ira Berkow, Red: A Biography of Red Smith ix (1986) (calling Smith "one of the best writers in the country, newspaper or otherwise"); Mark Bradley, *Sports In the Pandemic Era, and How We Cover Them Change*, Atlanta J.-Const., June 21, 2020 (calling Smith "the patron saint of sports writers").

[3]   Editors' Introduction, *Red Smith, Miracle of Coogan's Bluff*, in The Twentieth Century Treasury of Sports 592 (Al Silverman & Brian Silverman eds., 1992).

[4]   David Halberstam, *Introduction*, in The Best American Sports Writing of the Century xxx (David Halberstam ed., 1999); *see also* David Halberstam, *Introduction*, in Everything They Had: Sports Writing From David Halberstam 15 (Glenn Stout ed., 2008) (discussing "the fresh, graceful way [Smith] wrote").

[5]   Ira Berkow, *Red Smith*, in The New York Times Book of Sports Legends 316 (Joseph J. Vecchione ed., 1991).

[6]   Ira Berkow, *supra* note 2 at 246 (quoting Smith).

[7]   *Gulliver's Travels*, in Jonathan Swift, The Works of Jonathan Swift 304 (2d ed. 1883).

[8]   Charles Dickens, Bleak House 14 (1853) (Oxford U. Press 1976).

[9]   David Mellinkoff, The Language of the Law 193 (1963) (quoting Fielding).

[10]   Carl Sandburg, *Foreword*, in The Sandburg Range x (1957).

[11]   Nicholas Dawidoff (ed.), Baseball: An Anthology 102 (2002).

[12]   Carl Sandburg, *The Lawyers Know Too Much*, in Anthology of Mag. Verse for 1920 (William Stanley Braithwaite ed., 1920).

13   *Letter from Thomas Jefferson to Joseph Cabell* (Sept. 9, 1817), in 17 Writings of Thomas Jefferson 417–18 (Andrew A. Lipscomb ed., 1904).

14   Felix Frankfurter, *When Judge Cardozo Writes*, The New Republic, Apr. 8, 1931.

15   Fred Rodell, *Goodbye to Law Reviews*, 23 Va. L. Rev. 38, 38 (1936); *see also* Fred Rodell, *Goodbye to Law Reviews—Revisited*, 48 Va. L. Rev. 279 (1962).

16   Eugene C. Gerhart, *Improving Our Legal Writing: Maxims from the Masters*, 40 A.B.A. J. 1057, 1057 (1954).

17   Richard A. Posner, Divergent Paths 334 (2016); *see also, e.g.*, Stanard v. Nygren, 658 F.3d 792, 798 n.7 (7th Cir. 2011) (reciting "the unfortunate reality that poor writing occurs too often in our profession"); Joseph Kimble, *Introduction*, in Joseph Kimble, Lifting the Fog of Legalese: Essays on Plain Language xi (2006) ("[M]ost legal writing is bad and has been for centuries; most lawyers recognize this failing from what they read. . . .").

18   Jay Wishingrad & Douglas E. Abrams, *The Lawyer's Bookshelf*, N.Y.L.J., Dec. 12, 1980, at 2 (reviewing Richard C. Wydick, Plain English For Lawyers (1979)).

19   Felix Frankfurter & Harry Shulman, Cases and Other Authorities on Federal Jurisdiction and Procedure vii (rev. ed. 1937, reprinting *Introduction to Original Edition* (1931)).

20   Harry Kalven, Jr., *Law School Training in Research and Exposition: The University of Chicago Program*, 1 J. Legal Educ. 107, 108 (1948).

21   *E.g.*, Douglas E. Abrams, *Integrating Legal Writing Into Civil Procedure*, 24 Conn. L. Rev. 813, 814–45 & n.5 (1992); Gerald Lebovits, *Legal Writing in the Practice-Ready Law School*, N.Y. St. Bar Assoc. J.72, 72 (Sept. 2013).

22   Tom Goldstein & Jethro K. Lieberman, The Lawyer's Guide to Writing Well 8 (1989); Jay Wishingrad & Douglas E. Abrams, *supra* note 18.

23   *E.g.*, David Segal, *What They Don't Teach Law Students: Lawyering*, N.Y. Times, Nov. 20, 2011, at A1.

24   *E.g.*, Catherine H. Finn & Claudia Diamond, *Are We Listening?*, 29 Wash. Law. 27, 29 (Jan. 2015).

25   Abraham Lincoln, *Second Lecture on Discoveries and Inventions* 4 (Feb. 11, 1859), http://www.abrahamlincolnonline.org/lincoln/speeches/discoveries.htm (emphasis in original) (visited Aug. 10, 2020).

26   Stephen King, On Writing: A Memoir of the Craft 180 (2000).

CHAPTER 2

BASIC STRATEGIES

■ ■ ■

"[W]ritings are useless unless they are read," said President Theodore Roosevelt, "and they cannot be read unless they are readable."[1] Roosevelt wrote 13 books before he became President, and another 23 during and after his presidency.[2] He knew what he was talking about.

The quest for readable legal writing is not shrouded in mystery. The English language knows only two types of writing—good writing and bad writing. Good legal writing is good writing about a legal subject.[3] "[T]here's not some special magic about legal writing," says Justice Elena Kagan. "To be a good legal writer . . . is to know the law and be a good writer."[4]

The four fundamentals of good legal writing, grouped by Professor Henry Weihofen more than a generation ago, are conciseness, precision, simplicity, and clarity.[5] Commentators have embraced this quartet,[6] which Chapter 5 explores.

Professor Richard C. Wydick links the fundamentals with the realities of law practice by quoting a well-known New York attorney. "Good legal writing does not sound as though it had been written by a lawyer," the attorney would tell his firm's young associates.[7] "[G]ood legal writing," Professor Wydick adds, "should not differ, without good reason, from ordinary well-written English."[8]

This chapter presents 12 threshold strategies that, from the start of a writing project, remain central to good writing. Because these basic strategies support good writing generally, they support good legal writing.

"GOOD WRITING COMES FROM GOOD READING"[9]

In 1954, a 12-year-old junior high schooler wrote to Justice Felix Frankfurter seeking advice about how to prepare to become a lawyer.[10] "The best way to prepare for the law," Justice Frankfurter answered, "is to come to the study of law as a well-read person."[11] He advised that reading enables lawyers-to-be to "acquire the capacity to use the English language on paper and in speech and with the habits of clear thinking."[12]

This first basic strategy means reading not only for content, but also for style. Reading as a tool for developing one's own writing ability need not cease when a student receives the J.D. because a lawyer's quest for improved writing skills remains a lifelong work in progress, an apprenticeship as Hemingway put it.

Non-lawyers echo Justice Frankfurter with sage advice for writers of all ages. Henry David Thoreau called reading a "noble intellectual exercise,"[13] and Theodore Roosevelt attested that "I am a part of everything I have read."[14] In our own time, J.K. Rowling, author of the popular Harry Potter series, advises aspiring writers to "read as much as you can, like I did. It will give you an understanding of what makes good writing and it will enlarge your vocabulary."[15]

Reading makes a difference because literary classics and quality contemporary writings have generally withstood commentary and critique. Chapter 1 introduced a few prominent writers who likely never saw the inside of a law school classroom, and this chapter and later ones will introduce still more. Their example can influence law students and lawyers because the rules of good writing remain universal.

What about older readings whose wordy, circuitous, or otherwise troublesome styles seem alien to contemporary eyes and ears? Even these readings can yield valuable lessons by demonstrating how *not* to write today. As in many other areas of everyday life, a person can learn from others' failures as well as from their successes.

Few lawyers can forget, for example, their 1L struggles with *Pennoyer v. Neff,* the Supreme Court's landmark 1878 personal jurisdiction decision.[16] A survey of historians named *Pennoyer* the twelfth most influential decision in the Court's history,[17] but this lofty ranking leaves undiminished the contemporary reader's discomfort with extracting bedrock constitutional doctrine that Justice Stephen J. Field could have expressed more concisely, precisely, simply, and clearly.

MAINTAIN COMMITMENT

Good legal writing depends on unstinting personal and professional commitment to quality. "Writing well is hard," says journalist Tom Verducci. "It requires constant thinking. The gears, flywheels and levers of the mind click and clatter non-stop. Writing is flying an airplane without instruments, almost always through the dark storms of doubt. It is new every time."[18]

Navigating the dark storms of doubt may demand special self-discipline from lawyers, who normally write without pure freedom to explore subjects that stimulate our interest. Freedom of choice, the literary adrenaline that sustains many committed writers, may be an early casualty of a legal writing project done on a client's behalf.

Award-winning NBC journalist Edwin Newman explained the secret of his success: "You choose subjects that interest you, those that have a proven appeal, those on which you think you write well. . . . [I]n the final analysis, you write for yourself."[19] Sportswriter and novelist Frank Deford agreed that "you write best when you like your subject matter."[20]

In advocacy and counseling alike, however, lawyers usually do not write for ourselves, but rather as the representative of someone else, typically the private or public client. Representation means that lawyers frequently write about subjects that we would not have chosen of our own accord—subjects that might not interest us, or that might draw our ambivalence or even distaste. We sometimes write for clients or superiors we find difficult or may not know very well, and we sometimes take positions we would not take if we were (in Newman's words) writing for ourselves.

Regardless of a lawyer's personal feelings, however, producing the best possible writing remains a professional responsibility taken seriously by lawyers who remain mindful of their special role in the civil and criminal justice systems. Readers can often distinguish between legal writing that shines, and legal writing that appears dry and listless.

LIVE WITH THE PROJECT

"The best time for planning a book is when you're doing the dishes," said mystery writer Agatha Christie.[21] Personal and professional commitment to quality means that, except perhaps when facing a close deadline, a lawyer may begin to "write" by mulling over the project before ever composing anything. Other matters may compete for the lawyer's time and attention, but early planning means contemplating structure, concepts, and ideas.

Contemplation continues as the writing project proceeds because inspiration can come when least expected. "Write down the thoughts of the moment," instructed Sir Francis Bacon, because thoughts that "come unsought are commonly the most valuable and should be secured, because they seldom return."[22] During a writing assignment earlier in my career, I would keep a pen and pad on the night table near the bed because thoughts that occurred to me at 3 a.m. might slip from memory by morning. During the day, I would carry a pen and small pad in my pocket wherever I went. I might walk or jog on neighborhood streets, but I would stop to jot down words, phrases, or thoughts that might later escape me if I depended entirely on memory. Nowadays I carry a phone in my pocket, ready to text, email, or dictate into my home or office with ideas or passages I may want to use.

Lawyers might never bill clients for time spent collecting thoughts that occur intermittently during daily activities in or out of the office, perhaps even when the lawyer does the dishes. But clients deserve effective writing from lawyers who feel a sense of professional obligation to go the extra mile, to do what it takes. Without letting writing consume a well-rounded life, serious writers recognize that they are not "off-duty" when a writing project beckons.

CREATE A SCHEDULE

By focusing on the writing process generally, this book does not distinguish between lawyers who research and write alone, and lawyers who research and write as a team. The team approach prevails, for example, in a law firm when a partner assembles one or more associates on a project. The partner is the quarterback with ultimate responsibility for progress toward the goal line, the polished writing.

In solitary writing and team writing alike, lawyers frequently face tight deadlines imposed by courts, clients, or circumstances beyond the lawyer's control. Exigencies may mean writing as swiftly as possible, but legal writers otherwise manage impending deadlines best by setting an early, firm, but flexible schedule.

The schedule may evolve as the project itself evolves and new sources, authorities, and arguments emerge. But even with the prospect of change, early schedules identify threshold questions such as these: "By what date should I finish initial research?" "When should my tentative outline be ready?" "When should I begin writing the first draft?" "When should the workable first draft be ready?" "When should I begin enlisting editors' input?" and "When should cite-checking and other proofreading begin?"

A tentative schedule can serve worthwhile purposes:

1.   *Scheduling can help manage uncertainty.* "[F]ear is at the root of most bad writing," says novelist Stephen King. "If one is writing for one's own pleasure, that fear may be mild. . . . [I]f, however, one is working under deadline . . . that fear may be intense."[23] Fear and expressive dexterity do not easily mix, and even flexible schedules, subject to adaptation and change, can encourage early confidence and reassurance.

2.   *Scheduling can leave time to pursue unanticipated avenues.* Poet and baseball fan Marianne Moore likened poetry to baseball because "[y]ou can never tell with either how it will go or what you will do."[24] Experienced lawyers know that sooner or later, their researching and writing often point in directions initially unknown. Mindful of deadlines, generous initial scheduling leaves the writer time to abandon early leads and research unanticipated ones.

3.   *Scheduling may allow one or more temporary respites.* Sometimes the best way to write is to reserve some time not to write. If time constraints permit, lawyers living with a writing project can sometimes

avoid "mental overload" by stepping away from the keyboard for a day or more, collecting thoughts, and clearing the cobwebs before returning with a fresher perspective and a clearer outlook.

4.   *Scheduling leaves time for thorough, meaningful editing and proofreading.* Editors and proofreaders are busy people whose service the writer should not take for granted. Like the writer, editors need adequate time to scrutinize substance and style as the deadline approaches. Once editors weigh in, the writer needs time to evaluate their input and incorporate useful suggestions into the final product.

5.   *Scheduling can leave time to burnish the near-final product.* Now that personal computers make continual editing and touch-up so tempting, writing often expands to fit the time available. If a few days or even a few hours remain near a writing project's deadline, however, a resourceful lawyer can put the time to good use, either on the writing itself or on another matter. Burnishing a near-final draft can enhance quality, but feverish eleventh-hour editing can leave the lawyer at the mercy of the clock, which may run out before the final product emerges as free as possible from errors uncaught.

At some point near the end, editing must stop and the document must be readied for submission. When prudent scheduling avoids a last-minute frenzy, writers can better determine this point. "Haste makes waste" goes the adage, which remains a sound guidepost for legal writers.

WRITE AN OUTLINE

At final examination time each semester, law students learn first-hand that effective writing begins with a good written outline. If the professor allots two hours for an exam essay, for example, some students begin feverishly reading the fact pattern and writing answers from the opening moments. The more verbiage, the better—or so the students think. These students would be much better off spending a healthy portion of the allotted time outlining their anticipated points, and then working from the outline.

Practicing lawyers do not write final examinations, but the value of beginning with an organized outline remains. In *The Elements of Style*, William Strunk Jr. and E.B. White advised that "in most cases, planning must be a deliberate prelude to writing."[25] Outlining takes time but, similar to prudent businesspeople who "spend money to make money," prudent writers spend time to make time. By sharpening the writer's thought processes throughout the project, the early outline saves time by mapping a more coherent path.

Even if the writer initially does not know much about the expected subject matter, the best possible skeletal outline paves the way to the destination. List key points and sub-points, and then step away for a reasonable period if time permits. Reread the outline to identify gaps in the thought process. Perhaps confer with colleagues and other potential editors whose early input can pay rich dividends.

Keep the outline handy, and continue filling in gaps as researching and writing proceed. Re-order point headings and sub-headings to reflect new research and new ideas. Add new point headings and sub-headings as appropriate, and delete or edit others when they no longer seem suitable.

Writing, said author John Updike, "educates the writer as it goes along."[26] Poet Robert Frost acknowledged that "I have never started a poem yet whose end I knew. Writing a poem is discovering."[27] So is writing prose.

KNOW THE AUDIENCE

Journalist Christopher Hitchens encouraged writers to visualize themselves as striving to fulfill a contract with their readers.[28] To help deliver a message that connects, a legal writer must strive to Know the Audience, the other contracting parties.[29] "Who is likely to read this?" The answer may be well within the lawyer's grasp because much legal writing targets a discrete group readily identifiable in advance. The lawyer may even know the prospective readers personally, or else by name or reputation.[30]

Advocates know, for example, that briefs and similar submissions typically target the client, the parties, and the court but hardly anyone else. A judicial opinion usually speaks first to the parties, and later to future courts and litigants under our system of precedent. Sometimes, however, the writer can predict an even wider initial audience. For example, a writing by an advocate or judge may attract media attention if the writing concerns a public issue or a well-known person.[31]

A newspaper column, law review or bar journal article, or blog entry anticipates an audience of unknown readers. Often, however, the lawyer can foresee the readers' essential perspectives.

Professor Weihofen's four fundamentals of effective legal writing—conciseness, precision, simplicity, and clarity—remain universal, but the lawyer's tone may differ from audience to audience. The writing may seek to persuade, move, explain, or challenge. Predictions about readers' circumstances and anticipated reactions help set the appropriate tone. Will the audience likely be antagonistic or cooperative? An invitation to action, for example, may summon reactions different from those summoned by an adversarial brief.

Knowing the audience may also influence substantive explanation. Suppose, for example, that a tort lawyer writes about causation, a term whose legal meaning normally does not roll off laypersons' lips. Other tort lawyers need less explanation than lay clients, who may need less than teens in a high school civics class. Analysis that resonates with one audience may escape another. Readers trained in the law can also better digest unexplained terms of art (such as causation itself, whose doctrine might be intimately familiar to tort lawyers, less familiar to lawyers specializing in other fields, and entirely unfamiliar to high schoolers).

MASTER THE "LEGAL WRITER'S THEATER"

"[E]very trial is theater and every trial lawyer is a producer of a good, bad or indifferent play," instructed former federal district judge Simon H. Rifkind, a pillar of the New York Bar for nearly half a century.[32]

Trial lawyers are not the only bar members who perform to audiences. Lawyers appear on stage whenever we write for others. In physical dimensions, the Legal Writer's Theater—typically the office—is much smaller than a conventional theater, but size is no matter. Two-time Pulitzer Prize-winning historian David McCullough says that "[n]othing good was ever written in a large room."[33]

"All the world's a stage," Shakespeare wrote in *As You Like It*.[34] All the legal world certainly is. The Legal Writer's Theater is virtual because the lawyer typically sits at the keyboard without engaging readers face to face. The audience members—the readers who later digest the written words—nonetheless remain as central to the performance as an audience sitting in the orchestra or balcony. Educator and theatrical coach Viola Spolin was right that "[t]he audience is the most revered member of the theater. . . . They are our . . . evaluators and the last spoke in the wheel which can then begin to roll."[35]

Theater companies typically perform plays written earlier, but the stage performance is oral. Perhaps the force of oral performance is one reason why some commentators urge lawyers and other writers to read their early drafts aloud.[36] A biographer explains that the eloquent Abraham Lincoln "wrote for the ear. Most politicians and academics write for the eye. Lincoln often spoke or whispered out loud before putting his Faber pencil to paper. He was fascinated by the sound of words."[37]

Lincoln doubtlessly knew that by enlisting a second sense, oral rendition can enhance persuasion and help lawyers flag such shortcomings as flawed analysis and argumentation, convoluted sentences, inadvertently omitted words, and typographical errors. Because readers eventually "hear" what the lawyer enables them to hear, writing for the ear also lets the lawyer set the tone, which may remain cooperative, challenging, informational, or adversarial.

EARN THE RIGHT TO A READER

Just because a writer puts something down on paper does not necessarily mean that people will read it, wholly or even in large part. This frank recognition, drawn from humility and not from a sense of entitlement to an audience, led Catherine Drinker Bowen to post a simple sign above her desk as she wrote her well-crafted biographies: "Will the reader turn the page?"[38]

Audience members are more likely to turn the page when the writer takes affirmative steps to Earn the Right to a Reader. Similar to most other rights that must be earned, this one demands commitment and careful attention.

Especially in litigation, some of the lawyer's readers remain an essentially captive audience because their clients' interests depend on digesting the entire writing, no matter how unpalatable the chore. But where the option to stop reading remains (as in an *amicus* brief addressing a court), legal writers can earn the right to a reader by adhering to the four fundamentals of good writing—conciseness, precision, simplicity, and clarity—and by avoiding barriers to effective written expression, including barriers that Part Five of this book discusses. Bowen understood that earning the right does not come from taking readers for granted.

In a theatrical performance, the troupe succeeds when the audience remains seated until the final curtain. Writers similarly succeed when readers remain engaged until the end. "I never feel my writing is born or has an independent existence," said historian Barbara W. Tuchman, "until it is read."[39]

Writing without readers is not writing. Writers without readers are not writers.

ORIENT THE AUDIENCE

Theatergoers typically know much less about the play than the actors who have rehearsed or performed it for weeks, months, or more. In the legal writer's theater, readers may similarly know much less about the relevant facts and law than the writer does, at least initially. The matter may concern a specialty familiar to the lawyer after years of experience. The lawyer may have lived with the matter while interviewing, researching, and writing. Whether readers are laypersons or trained in the law, they may enter the virtual theater as an uninitiated audience.

Unless the lawyer orients readers before proceeding very far, the lawyer risks confounding the audience early. Orienting may mean "frontloading"—opening a section, subsection, or other lengthy written exposition with a paragraph or two that summarizes the discussion that will follow. From there, orienting may depend on continued explanations responsive to the audience's circumstances.

Few readers need orientation more than judges, who candidly acknowledge that they may know much less about a case's law or facts than advocates assume they know at the beginning. "It is unhelpful," says one federal district judge, "when attorneys write briefs that presuppose specialized knowledge on the part of their readers."[40] Judge Posner confides that "judges do not feel patronized, or condescended to, when a lawyer explains in words of one syllable some scientific, technological, or other arcane feature of a case that is necessary to a full understanding. . . . The judges are happy to be educated by the lawyers in the intricacies of a case."[41]

If experienced judges near the legal profession's pinnacle depend on orientation from the writer, consider the plight of less experienced legally-trained readers, not to mention clients and laypersons whom the writing may seek to reach. When a lawyer denies readers a comprehensible early roadmap, the lawyer risks losing the audience.

USE FORMS CAREFULLY, IF AT ALL

Forms and internal form files have long been staples in private law firms and public agencies, and courts recognize that a lawyer who cuts-and-pastes from a prior brief, memorandum, or other hard copy or electronic form can avoid wasteful efforts to "reinvent the wheel." The lawyer profits from prior wisdom while conserving professional time, and thus presumably also reducing cost to the client.

A form remains useful, however, only when the lawyer carefully adapts it to suit the present matter. Cutting-and-pasting can be a tantalizing invitation to harmful corner-cutting. Form briefs and other court submissions (like form agreements and other non-litigation form documents) may appear grammatically correct and structurally sound, but they may carry unintended adverse consequences for failing to reflect the facts and law that will influence or determine the client's cause.

Whether created by the writer or by someone else, the form may have emerged from a context quite different from today's, though the difference may not be apparent from the face of the form months or years later. The form may have been developed or finalized under the law of a jurisdiction other than the one that would govern today's proceeding. Even within a particular jurisdiction, the dispositive law may have evolved or changed in the interim. The form may have emerged from negotiations unlike any negotiations that mark the present case.

The bottom line? Cutting-and-pasting from briefs, memoranda, and other prior sources can be efficient and productive when done carefully, but not as a shortcut or substitute for analysis, interpretation, and reasoning based on counsel's research and understanding of the present case's facts and law.

DELIVER CIVILITY AND PROFESSIONALISM

In 2011, American Bar Association President Stephen N. Zack decried the legal profession's "continuing slide into the gutter of incivility."[42] An ABA resolution that year "affirm[ed] the principle of civility as a foundation for democracy and the rule of law," and urged lawyers in their conduct and expression "to set a high standard for civil discourse as an example for others in resolving differences constructively and without disparagement of others."[43]

Later ABA presidents have reiterated the call for a high standard. In 2017, Linda A. Klein wrote that "[a]s leaders in society, lawyers must insure that civility once again becomes a quality that defines us."[44] In 2019, Bob Carlson also identified a leadership role: "Civility needs . . . to become part of our normal day-to-day interactions. Lawyers, as role models, have a special obligation to practice civility."[45]

The ABA's voice echoes federal and state courts that call lawyers' civil conduct and expression "a linchpin of our legal system,"[46] "a vital pillar in the justice system and our society,"[47] and "a hallmark of professionalism."[48] The California Court of Appeal says that lawyers' incivility "brings disrepute to the entire legal profession," and demonstrates "the kind of behavior the bench and bar together must continually strive to eradicate."[49]

Lawyers' civility also commands the attention of the nation's highest court. Justice Anthony M. Kennedy calls civility "the mark of an accomplished and superb professional" that "defines our common cause in advancing the rule of law."[50] Chief Justice Warren E. Burger called civility "the lubricant[] that prevent[s] lawsuits from turning into combat."[51] "Courtesy is an essential element of effective advocacy," agreed Justice John Paul Stevens.[52]

Chief Justice John G. Roberts, Jr. summoned civility during President Trump's impeachment proceedings in early 2020. With emotions running high in the well of the Senate in the wee hours of the morning, the Chief Justice admonished the House managers and the President's counsel that "they are addressing the world's greatest deliberative body. One reason it has earned that title is because its members avoid speaking in a manner and using language that is not conducive to civil discourse."[53]

These contemporary voices urging civility sound a venerable theme central to responsible written advocacy. In 1917, for example, an advocate recited the theme this way: "[I]n no case should a brief be used as a vehicle for conveying hatred, contempt, insult, disrespect, or professional discourtesy of any nature to the court of review, to the trial judge, or to opposing counsel."[54]

The adversary system's pressures can also strain the tone and tenor of a lawyer's oral speech, but the strain on civility can be especially great when lawyers write. Written words arrive without the tone of voice, facial expression, body language, or contemporaneous opportunity for explanation that can soothe face-to-face communication. Writing appears cold on the page, dependent not necessarily on what the writer intends or implies, but on what readers infer.

Incivility in writing may pit lawyer against lawyer, or it may pit lawyer against the court. Each of these two manifestations warrants a representative example here, followed by assessment of the damage that a lawyer's written incivility can inflict on clients, and on the lawyer's own personal fulfillment and professional career.

Lawyer-on-Lawyer Incivility

When Chief U.S. Bankruptcy Judge Terrence L. Michael (N.D. Okla.) considered whether to approve a compromise in *In re Gordon* (2013), the Chapter 7 proceeding detoured into written lawyer-on-lawyer invective.[55]

In a filing to support a motion to compel discovery from the bankruptcy trustee in *Gordon*, the lawyer for the creditor Commerce Bank charged that the trustee and the United States had engaged in "a pattern . . . to avoid any meaningful examination of the legal validity of the litigation plan they have concocted to bring . . . a series of baseless claims."[56]

"[T]hey know," the bank's lawyer continued, "that a careful examination of this process will show the several fatal procedural flaws that will prevent these claims from being asserted."[57] "Only by sweeping these issues under the rug will the Trustee be able to play his end game strategy of asserting wild claims . . . in hopes of coercing Commerce Bank into a settlement (which the Trustee hopes will generate significant contingency fees for himself)."[58]

The trustee charged that the bank's lawyer had impugned his character with accusations that he had compromised his fiduciary obligations for personal gain. Judge Michael denied the trustee's motion for sanctions on procedural grounds, but he chastised the bank's lawyer because "personal and vitriolic accusations have no place as part of a litigation strategy."[59] The court instructed the parties to "leave the venom at home,"[60] because "[w]hether you like (or get along well with) your opposition has little to do with the merits of a particular case."[61]

Sometimes citing the costs that lawyers' incivility can impose on the judicial system itself,[62] some courts have moved beyond instruction. Exercising inherent authority, these courts have sanctioned lawyers, struck pleadings, or denied attorneys' fees, for incivility.[63] Some courts have even sanctioned the client who, having retained the lawyer, may bear some responsibility for the lawyer's conduct.[64]

Lawyer-on-Court Incivility

Gordon's written recriminations pitted counsel against counsel, but lawyers sometimes stray into incivility that disrespects judges and the court. Judgments and appeals may involve at least one party who believes that the court reached an incorrect outcome, but few judges deserve criticism for incompetence.

A lawyer's criticism crossed the line during the federal district court's review of the magistrate judge's report and recommendation in *In re Photochromic Lens Antitrust Litigation*.[65] The lawyer contended that the magistrate judge was "misled" concerning relevant legal standards, and that the magistrate made her recommendation without "any reference to the voluminous underlying record." The lawyer further contended that the magistrate "conducted no analysis, much less a 'rigorous analysis,' " and decided "based on no evidence, a superficial misreading of the evidence, or highly misleading evidence."[66]

The district court approved the magistrate judge's recommendation and report in significant part, but did not stop there. The court's opinion also reprimanded the lawyer: "It is disrespectful and unbecoming of a lawyer to resort to such language, particularly when directed toward a judicial officer. Its use connotes arrogance, and reflects an unprofessional, if not immature litigation strategy of casting angry aspersions rather than addressing the merits . . . in a dignified and respectful manner."[67]

Incivility's Costs to the Client

A leading Supreme Court advocate described the stiff price a client may pay for its lawyer's descent into incivility. "The argument *ad hominem* in a brief is always unpardonable, not simply because it is something no decently constituted brief-writer would include, but because, like all other faults, it fails of its purpose," namely to persuade the decision maker.[68]

The Chief Justice of the Maine Supreme Judicial Court confides that "[a]s soon as I see an attack of any kind on the other party, opposing counsel, or the trial judge, I begin to discount the merits of the argument."[69] When determining the parties' rights and obligations by applying facts to law, perhaps judges sometimes react this way because civility projects strength and incivility projects weakness. "Rudeness is the weak man's imitation of strength," said philosopher Eric Hoffer.[70]

A lawyer's initial step toward civility may be an early candid talk with the client, who may assume that the surest path to victory is representation by an unleashed junkyard dog. The client's instincts may stem from movie and television dramas, whose portrayals of lawyers often sacrifice realism for entertainment.

Without this early candid talk, the client may mistake the lawyer's civility for meekness, and courtesy for concession. Avoiding such mistakes advances effective writing. "[C]ivility is not a sign of weakness," President John F. Kennedy reassured Americans in his Inaugural Address in 1961, as he anticipated four years of Cold War standoffs with the Soviets.[71] "Civility assumes that we will disagree," explains Yale law professor Stephen L. Carter. "[I]t requires us not to mask our differences but to resolve them respectfully."[72]

From the outset, the client needs to understand that a take-no-prisoners strategy can disgust any decision maker who shares the sensibilities expressed by the justices and judges quoted here. One Illinois state appellate judge says, "No judge has ever been heard to endorse or encourage the use [of mean-spirited] writing. Not one. You may feel better writing it and your client may feel better reading it, but your audience is the judge, and judges abhor it."[73] Arousing judicial abhorrence scores counsel or client no points.

Justice Sandra Day O'Connor explains that "[i]t is enough for the ideas and positions of the parties to clash; the lawyers don't have to."[74] "It isn't necessary to say anything nasty about your adversary or to make deriding comments about the opposing brief," adds Justice Ruth Bader Ginsburg, who says that such comments "are just distractions. You should aim to persuade the judge by the power of *your* reasoning and not by denigrating the opposing side. . . . If the other side is truly bad, the judges are smart enough to understand that themselves; they don't need the lawyer's aid."[75]

Judges are not alone in equating civility with strength. John W. Davis closed his career with 141 arguments before the Supreme Court, the most of any 20th century lawyer.[76] From rich experience, he knew the judicial audience. "[C]ontroversies between counsel," he wrote, "impose on the court the wholly unnecessary burden and annoyance of preserving order and maintaining the decorum of its proceedings. Such things can irritate, they can never persuade."[77]

Finally, there is the matter of avoidable expense today, when many Americans can barely afford legal representation, when institutional and individual clients reportedly scrutinize legal bills more closely than ever, and when law firms often outsource document review and similar legal work to reduce costs. "[I]ncivility disserves the client," says Justice O'Connor, "because it wastes time and energy—time that is billed to the client at hundreds of dollars an hour, and energy that is better spent working on the case than working over the opponent."[78]

Incivility's Costs to the Lawyer

Aside from threatening to compromise the client's interests, incivility can damage the lawyer's own personal satisfaction and professional standing. Incivility "takes the fun from the practice of law," says U.S. Circuit Judge Duane Benton.[79] "Being a lawyer can be pleasant or unpleasant," explains U.S. Circuit Judge William J. Bauer, who adds that "[w]hen we treat each other and those with whom we have professional contact with civility, patience and even kindness, the job becomes more pleasant and easier."[80]

As members of a largely self-regulated profession devoted to the rule of law, lawyers are judged by expectations sometimes even higher than the expectations that judge other citizens. The Preamble to the ABA Model Rules of Professional Conduct recites "the lawyer's obligation zealously to protect and pursue a client's legitimate interests, within the bounds of the law, while maintaining a professional, courteous and civil attitude toward all persons involved in the legal system."[81] Model Rule 8.4(d), which prohibits lawyers' conduct that is "prejudicial to the administration of justice," may support professional discipline arising from incivility.[82]

The Model Rules' spotlight on professional obligation is fortified by commands for civility in federal and state court rules,[83] state admissions oaths,[84] and unofficial codes that some professional organizations maintain for their member lawyers.[85] The ABA Model Code of Judicial Conduct imposes reciprocal obligations of civility on judges in the performance of their official duties.[86]

These professional commands and expectations mean that writing marred by incivility can damage the lawyer's reputation among judges and other lawyers. The damage seems greatest when the court's opinion calls out counsel publicly, either by name or by leaving counsel readily identifiable from the appearances atop the opinion. Offending counsel in the two decisions presented above, *In re Gordon* and *In re Photochromic Lens Antitrust Litigation*, may have had second thoughts when courts shined the spotlight on their shortcomings.

But even without public spotlight or evident disdain from the bench, word gets around. In cities, suburbs, and outstate areas alike, the bench and bar usually comprise relatively small groups bound by mutual relationships, word of mouth, recollections, and experience. Lawyers with reputations for civility stand a better chance of receiving civility in return. Sooner or later, for example, a lawyer may need a stipulation, consent to a continuance, or similar professional courtesy from an opponent or the court. Like other people, lawyers can expect to get what they give.

In a challenging employment market, a reputation for civility may even enhance a lawyer's professional mobility. Lawyers sometimes receive lateral job offers from a public- or private-sector adversary who respects not only their competence, but also their professionalism. Being smart is not enough. Plenty of lawyers are smart, but fewer lawyers earn abiding peer respect for an extra measure of professionalism as they advocate for their clients. Few Americans (including few lawyers) spend their entire careers with their first employer, so enhanced lateral mobility can be a significant reward for unswerving commitment to an honorable law practice.

Incivility brings tarnish, but civility brings luster. "Just as lawyers gossip about judges and most litigators have a 'book' on the performances of trial judges, we judges keep our own book on litigators who practice before us," confides one federal district judge.[87] Another veteran federal district judge links dexterity to civility: "The lawyers who are the most skillful tend to be reasonably civil lawyers because they project an image of self-confidence. They don't have to stoop to the level of acrimony."[88]

A Connecticut appellate judge advises advocates that "[y]our character may be the most effective means of persuasion you possess."[89] When I served as a judicial law clerk, I learned that when many judges pick up a brief or other submission, they look first for the writer's name and affiliation. A writer with a track record for civility and forthright, principled advocacy gets a head start; a writer who has previously fallen short must make up lost ground.

President Theodore Roosevelt said that "[c]ourtesy is as much a mark of a gentleman as courage."[90] "The greater man, the greater courtesy," wrote British Poet Laureate Alfred, Lord Tennyson in his epic poem, *Idylls of the King*.[91]

The greater lawyer too.

The Will to Win

"All advocacy involves conflict and calls for the will to win," said New Jersey Supreme Court Chief Justice Arthur T. Vanderbilt, but the will to win is only one ingredient of professionalism.[92] Advocates, he added, also "must have character," marked by "certain general standards of conduct, of manners, and of expression." In the adversary system of justice, civility under stress remains a prime marker of an advocate's character, essential to the repertoire of a professional who remains committed to the letter and spirit of the ABA Model Rules.[93]

Civility in advocacy resembles sportsmanship in athletics. Sportsmanship presumes that each athlete wants to win within the rules of the game; a sportsmanlike athlete who does not care about winning should not play. Civility similarly presumes that each advocate wants to win within the rules of professionalism; a civil advocate who does not care about winning should not represent a client or cause. Civility and forceful advocacy, like sportsmanship and forceful athleticism, define the total package.

DELIVER RESPECT

Intimately linked to civility is the final threshold strategy profiled here, writing that respects race, ethnicity, gender, sexual orientation, religion, disability or challenge, or other differences among identifiable groups in American society. Justice Kennedy draws the link: "Civility has deep roots in the idea of respect for the individual. We are civil to each other because we respect one another's human aspirations and equal standing in a democratic society."[94]

Respect remains a cornerstone of legal writing. The ABA Model Rules of Professional Conduct specify that the lawyer serves as "an officer of the legal system and a public citizen having special responsibility for the quality of justice."[95] The ABA Model Code of Judicial Conduct specifies that the judiciary "plays a central role in preserving the principles of justice and the rule of law."[96] Respectful writing by a lawyer or judge creates a permanent record of the writer's fidelity to these instructions.

As Professors Laurel Currie Oates and Anne Enquist advise, respect normally means identifying a group by a name commonly preferred by its members in everyday communication.[97] These preferences may change over time, and legal writers should recognize the dynamics of change.

In 2016, President Barack Obama signed H.R. 4238, which the House of Representatives and the Senate had each passed unanimously.[98] The bipartisan bill amended two acts that, written in the 1970s, referred to persons by such then-prevailing names as Negro, American Indian, Oriental, Eskimo, and Aleut. H.R. 4238 struck these names and substituted ones such as African American, Native American, Asian American, Hispanic, Pacific Islander, and Alaska Native.[99]

In an age when fierce partisanship divides both houses of Congress, the unanimous passage of H.R. 4238 should influence drafters of federal or state legislation and administrative regulations. The bill should also influence lawyers and judges who write in such contexts as private- and public-sector advocacy or in court opinions.

Acknowledging generational change through respectful identification leaves uninhibited the writer's opportunity to vigorously argue substantive or procedural positions on the merits, whether pro or anti, liberal or conservative, or otherwise. Two examples—race and gender—make the point.

Race

Over time, "colored" has yielded to "Negro," which has yielded to "Black" or "person of color" or "African American." Lawyers ordinarily should use a commonly preferred identifier. In appropriate contexts, however, writers should leave well-known historical terms untouched, including terms whose expression would be unacceptable on a clean slate today. Remaining untouched, for example, are such historical names as the Negro Leagues, the black or African American professional baseball organizations during Major League Baseball's Jim Crow era.

Gender

Backed by equal protection doctrine and general social expectations, contemporary American law broadly rejects officially sanctioned gender discrimination. Gone too are the days when legal writers could expect readers routinely to accept, tacitly or explicitly, that "the masculine includes the feminine." Federal and state codes typically retain such gender-neutralizing ground rules in their general-construction provisions,[100] but legislative and administrative drafters are inching toward gender neutrality in future enactments and amendments.

The English language has no third-person singular pronouns that encompass both genders. Depending on the context, writers can consider familiar constructions that avoid gender bias. Professor Wydick and others advance several that appear here.[101]

One such construction uses unitary third-party plural pronouns ("Every law student must do *his* best" becomes "Law students must do *their* best."). Sometimes the message needs no pronoun at all ("Success in law school depends on students' best efforts."). As sometimes more awkward fallback positions, the lawyer can try alternating masculine and feminine pronouns from one passage to the next, or using a "his or her" construction ("Every law student must do *his or her* best.").

Using "s/he" or "he/she" seems stilted and can usually be avoided with one of the alternative constructions just mentioned. Also often avoidable are constructions that mix singular and plural constructions ("*Each* law student must do *their* best," becomes "Law students must do their best."). Recent trends suggest, however, that using "they" as a third-person singular pronoun continues to gain greater acceptance.[102]

Gender neutrality also means eliminating gender-based identifiers (for example, "businessman" becomes "businessperson"), and identifiers that denigrate one gender. In formal writing, it may be appropriate to use the term "girl" or "young woman" to identify a female who is in high school or younger, provided that the writing refers to similarly situated males as "boys" or "young men." But the term "woman" (and not "girl" or "gal") describes an older female, and "man" (and not "boy" or "guy") describes an older male.

Also instructive here is the earlier discussion about leaving well-known historical terms untouched in contemporary racial identification. In appropriate contexts, writers should similarly leave untouched gendered historical expression that might raise eyebrows today. A few pages ago, the discussion of civility quoted British Poet Laureate Alfred, Lord Tennyson: "The greater man, the greater courtesy." The discussion did not modernize the quote with brackets ("The greater [person], the greater courtesy."). The discussion trusted audience members to draw their own conclusions about the source and the expression, discernment within the capacities of most readers.

Simply Correct

Racial and ethnic minorities, women, persons with disabilities, and members of other groups concerned about their appropriate identification comprise a bulk of lawyers, clients, judges, witnesses, and others in everyday life. From a practical standpoint, respectful identification can encourage readers to respect the writer, and thus the writer's message. An inappropriate identifier from a lawyer or judge may rankle readers, and thus may deflect attention from the writer's substantive or procedural message. Respectful writing stands a much better chance of focusing attention where it belongs—on the writer's argument, persuasiveness, and position on the merits.

Words and names matter. Despite some lingering cynics, we should not belittle respectful writing as "politically correct," or "PC." The social fabric emerges stronger when writing by legal professionals respects personal dignity. Respect is not "politically" correct; it is simply correct.

---

[1]   Theodore Roosevelt, *History as Literature, Presidential Address to the American Historical Association—1912,* https://www.historians.org/about-aha-and-membership/aha-history-and-archives/presidential-addresses/theodore-roosevelt (visited Aug. 10, 2020).

[2]   Theodore Roosevelt Ctr., *Books Written by Theodore Roosevelt,* http://www.theodore rooseveltcenter.org/Research/Digital-Library/Record.aspx?libID=o274790 (visited Aug. 10, 2020).

[3]   Jay Wishingrad & Douglas E. Abrams, *The Lawyer's Bookshelf,* N.Y.L.J., Dec. 12, 1980, at 2 (reviewing Richard C. Wydick, Plain English For Lawyers (1st ed. 1979)).

[4]   Justice Elena Kagan, *Interview With Bryan A. Garner,* www.lawprose.org (video, part 2) (July 15, 2015).

[5]   Henry Weihofen, Legal Writing Style 4, 8–104 (2d ed. 1980); Antonio Gidi & Henry Weihofen, Legal Writing Style (3d ed. 2018).

[6]   *E.g.,* David Mellinkoff, Legal Writing: Sense and Nonsense xvii–xxvii (1982); Jim McElhaney, *Listen to What You Write,* 97 A.B.A. J. 20 (Jan. 2011); Charles R. Calleros, Legal Method and Writing 3–4 (5th ed. 2006); Richard K. Neumann, Jr. & Kristen Konrad Tiscione, Legal Reasoning and Legal Writing 6 (7th ed. 2013).

[7]   Richard C. Wydick, Plain English For Lawyers 4 (5th ed. 2005).

[8]   *Id.*

[9]   Charles Kuralt, Larry King Live, Nov. 1, 1990 (interviewing Kuralt).

[10]   Felix Frankfurter, *Advice to a Young Person Interested in a Career in the Law,* https://betterchancery.com/2010/07/20/advice-to-a-young-person-interested-in-a-career-in-the-law/ (visited Aug. 10, 2020).

[11]   *Id.*

[12]   *Id.*

13   Henry David Thoreau, *Walden*, in Works of Henry David Thoreau 116 (Lily Owens ed., 1981).

14   James G. Stavridis, *Read, Think, Write: Keys to 21st-Century Security Leadership*, Joint Force Q., Oct. 2011, at 111 (quoting President Roosevelt).

15   *They Said It*, The Sunday Mail (Queensland, Australia), Feb. 24, 2013, at 6 (quoting Rowling).

16   95 U.S. 714 (1878).

17   Montgomery N. Kosma, *Measuring the Influence of Supreme Court Justices*, 27 J. Legal Stud. 333, 359 tbl. 6 (1998).

18   Tom Verducci, *The Passion of Roger Angell*, Sports Illustrated, July 21, 2014, at 54, 62.

19   Edwin Newman, I Must Say: Edwin Newman on English, the News, and Other Matters xiv–xv, xviii (1989).

20   Frank Deford, Over Time: My Life as a Sportswriter 127 (2012).

21   *Riding the Rails With Agatha*, Edmonton J. (Canada), Nov. 10, 2017 (quoting Christie).

22   David Young, Breakthrough Power for Leaders: A Daily Guide to an Extraordinary Life 58 (2011) (quoting Bacon).

23   Stephen King, On Writing: A Memoir of the Craft 127 (2000).

24   Marianne Moore, *Baseball and Writing*, in Baseball: A Literary Anthology 349 (Nicholas Dawidoff ed., 2002).

25   William Strunk Jr. & E.B. White, The Elements of Style 15 (4th ed. 2000).

26   *John Updike, in* Encyclopedia of the Essay 868 (Tracy Chevalier ed., 1997).

27   Dick Mason, *Poetry Contest Winners Earn Accolades*, The Observer (La Grande, Oregon), May 23, 2012 (quoting Robert Frost).

28   Brian Lamb, *Christopher Hitchens*, in Booknotes: America's Finest Authors on Reading, Writing, and the Power of Ideas 254 (1997).

29   *E.g.*, Jay Wishingrad & Douglas E. Abrams, *Book Review*, 1981 Duke L.J. 1061, 1065 (reviewing George D. Gopen, Writing From a Legal Perspective (1981)).

30   Henry Weihofen, *supra* note 5 at 6; Antonio Gidi & Henry Weihofen, *id.*

31   *Compare* Lee C. Bollinger, Images of a Free Press 42 (1991) (the Supreme Court "can perform a deeply educative role in society, affecting behavior far beyond the strictly legal domain"), *with* William H. Rehnquist, *Act Well Your Part: Therein All Honor Lies*, 7 Pepperdine L. Rev. 227, 227–28 (1980) ("[T]he Supreme Court does not 'teach' in the normal sense of that word at all. In many cases we hand down decisions which we believe are required by some Act of Congress or some provision of the Constitution for which we, as citizens, might have very little sympathy and would not choose to make a rule of law if it were left solely to us.").

32   Debra Whitefield, *Simon Rifkind Takes On the $11-Billion Case*, L.A. Times, July 28, 1986, pt. 4, at 1 (quoting Judge Rifkind).

33   *Interview by Elizabeth Gaffney & Benjamin Ryder Howe with David McCullough, The Art of Biography No. 2* (Fall 1999), http://www.theparisreview.org/interviews/894/the-art-of-biography-no-2-david-mccullough (visited Aug. 10, 2020).

34   William Shakespeare, *As You Like It*, act 2, sc. 7, in William Shakespeare, The Complete Works 622 (Dorset Press 1988).

35   Viola Spolin, Improvisation for the Theater: A Handbook of Teaching and Directing Techniques 12–13 (1963).

36   *E.g.*, William Zinsser, On Writing Well 36–37 (2001); Jim McElhaney, *Listen to What You Write*, 97 A.B.A. J. 20 (Jan. 2011); Benjamin Dreyer, Dreyer's English: An Utterly Correct Guide to Clarity and Style 7 (2019).

37   Ronald C. White, Jr., The Eloquent President: A Portrait of Lincoln Through His Words xxii (2005).

38   Ruggero J. Aldisert et al., *Opinion Writing and Opinion Readers*, 31 Cardozo L. Rev. 1, 39 n.87 (2009).

39   Barbara W. Tuchman, Practicing History 81 (1981).

40   Waddy v. Globus Medical, Inc., No. 407CV075, 2008 WL 3861994 *2 n.4 (S.D. Ga. Aug. 18, 2008).

41   Richard A. Posner, Divergent Paths 188 (2016).

⁴²   James Podgers (ed.), *From Many Voices, a Call for Public Civility*, 97 A.B.A. J. 58 (Sept. 2011) (quoting Zack).

⁴³   *ABA Res. 108* (adopted by the House of Delegates (Aug. 2011)), bit.ly/ABARes108.

⁴⁴   Linda A. Klein, *One Word: Civility*, 103 A.B.A. J. 8 (Feb. 2017) (President's Message).

⁴⁵   Bob Carlson, *Looking Ahead to 2019*, 105 A.B.A. J. 8 (Jan.–Feb. 2019) (President's Message).

⁴⁶   Wilson v. Airtherm Prods., Inc., 436 F.3d 906, 912 n.5 (8th Cir. 2006).

⁴⁷   Oquendo v. Costco Wholesale Corp., No. 17-2238, 2020 WL 1698991 at *3 (D.P.R. Apr. 7, 2020).

⁴⁸   Cardello v. Cardello, No. FA020088156S, 2002 WL 31875435, at *1 (Conn. Super. Ct. Dec. 4, 2002).

⁴⁹   Finton Constr., Inc. v. Bidna & Keys, APLC, 190 Cal. Rptr.3d 1, 5 (Ct. App. 2015).

⁵⁰   Louis H. Pollak, *Professional Attitude*, 84 A.B.A. J. 66 (Aug. 1998) (quoting Justice Kennedy).

⁵¹   Warren E. Burger, *The Necessity for Civility*, 52 F.R.D. 211, 214–15 (1971).

⁵²   Marvin E. Aspen, *Let Us Be "Officers of the Court,"* 83 A.B.A. J. 94 (July 1997) (quoting Justice Stevens).

⁵³   Richard Wolf, *In Trump's Senate Impeachment Trial, Chief Justice John Roberts Enforces Civility*, USA TODAY, Jan, 24, 2020.

⁵⁴   Orrin N. Carter, *Preparation and Presentation of Cases in Courts of Review*, 12 Ill. L. Rev. 147, 152 (1917).

⁵⁵   484 B.R. 825 (Bankr. N.D. Okla. 2013).

⁵⁶   *Id.* at 827.

⁵⁷   *Id.*

⁵⁸   *Id.* at 827–28.

⁵⁹   *Id.* at 828.

⁶⁰   *Id.* at 830–31.

⁶¹   *Id.* at 830.

⁶²   *See, e.g.,* Oquendo, *supra* note 49 at *2.

⁶³   G.M. Filisko, *You're Out of Order! Dealing with the Costs of Incivility in the Legal Profession*, 99 A.B.A. J., Jan. 2013, at 55; Wescott Agri-Prods., Inc. v. Sterling State Bank, Inc., 682 F.3d 1091, 1095–96 (8th Cir. 2012); Oquendo, *supra* note 47 at *3.

⁶⁴   *E.g.,* Wescott Agri-Prods., Inc., *supra* note 63 at 1096.

⁶⁵   No. 2173, 2014 WL 1338605 (M.D. Fla. Apr. 3, 2014).

⁶⁶   *Id.* at *1 n.1.

⁶⁷   *Id. See also, e.g.* Board of Prof'l Responsibility v. Parrish, 556 S.W.3d 153, 157–58 (Tenn. 2018) (suspending for six months the lawyer who, on a recusal motion, accused the intermediate appellate court panel of, among other things, "rigging the game" and issuing an opinion that included the panel's "convenient and illegitimately purposeful fabrication").

⁶⁸   Frederick Bernays Wiener, Briefing and Arguing Federal Appeals § 83, at 258 (1961).

⁶⁹   Leigh Ingalls Saufley, *Amphibians and Appellate Courts*, 51 Me. L. Rev. 18, 23 (1999); *see also, e.g.,* State Compensation Ins. Fund v. Drobot, No. SACV 13-0956, 2016 WL 6661338, at *2 (C.D. Cal. Aug. 10, 2016) ("a civil tone can buy credibility with the court"); Turner v. Chipotle Mex. Grill, Inc., No. 14-cv-2612, 2015 WL 5579579, at *3 (D. Colo. Sept. 23, 2015) (in defense counsel's motion papers, "sarcasm and insult demonstrate[d] more than a lack of civility; they represent[ed] a failure of persuasion").

⁷⁰   Eric Hoffer, The Passionate State of Mind: And Other Aphorisms 100 (2006).

⁷¹   John F. Kennedy Presidential Lib. & Museum, *Inaugural Address, 20 Jan. 1961. See also, e.g.,* Heidi K. Brown, *Civility Reboot: Can Lawyers Learn to Be Nicer to One Another?*, 104 A.B.A. J. 22 (Oct. 2018) ("civility is not weakness").

⁷²   Stephen L. Carter, Civility 132 (1998).

⁷³   Naomi Kogan Dein, *The Need for Civility in Legal Writing*, 21 CBA Record 55 (Feb./Mar. 2007) (quoting Judge Michael B. Hyman).

⁷⁴   Sandra Day O'Connor, *Professionalism*, 76 Wash. U. L.Q. 5, 9 (1998).

[75]   *Interviews with United States Supreme Court Justices Conducted by Bryan A. Garner: Justice Ruth Bader Ginsburg,* 13 Scribes J. Legal Writing 142 (2010) (quoting Justice Ginsburg) (italics in original).

[76]   *Listening to John W. Davis,* 3 J. App. Practice and Process 743, 744 (2001).

[77]   John W. Davis, *The Argument of an Appeal,* 26 A.B.A. J. 895, 898 (1940); *see also, e.g.,* Nissim Corp. v. Clearplay, Inc., 499 Fed. Appx. 23, 27 n.4 (Fed. Cir. 2012) (unpublished opinion) (name calling in both parties' briefs made the submissions "difficult to take seriously and unpleasant to read").

[78]   Sandra Day O'Connor, *Professionalism,* 76 Wash. U. L.Q. 5, 9 (1998) (emphasis in original).

[79]   Duane Benton, *Chief Justice's Address to Members of the Missouri Bar*, Sept. 24, 1998, 54 J. Mo. Bar 302, 302 (1998).

[80]   J. Timothy Eaton, *Civility, Judge Bauer and the CBA,* 28 CBA Record 8 (Feb.–Mar. 2014) (quoting Judge Bauer). *See also, e.g.,* State Compensation Ins. Fund, *supra* note 71 at *2 (C.D. Cal. Aug. 10, 2016) (lawyers' incivility "mak[es] the practice of the profession unnecessarily miserable").

[81]   ABA Model Rules of Prof'l Conduct Preamble [9] (2019). *See also, e.g.,* In re Generic Pharmaceuticals Pricing Antitrust Litigation, No. 16-MD-2724, 2019 WL 6044308, at *1 n.4 (E.D. Pa. Oct. 7, 2019) (criticizing incivility that marked some of the parties' briefs; "Counsel may disagree strongly and in good faith without devolving into acrimony.")

[82]   ABA Model Rules of Prof'l Conduct 8.4(d); *see, e.g.,* In re Halpin, 53 N.E.3d 405 (Ind. 2015) (for violating Rule 8.4(d), suspending for not less than 60 days, without automatic reinstatement, lawyer whose motion papers accused the trial judge of taking a "stubbornly injudicious attitude," and of "taking off on detours and frolics that ignore the fact that there are laws in Indiana that the court is supposed to follow and uphold").

[83]   *See Lawyers' Duties to the* Court, Standards for Prof'l Conduct Within the 7th Cir. R. 1 (2020).

[84]   G.M. Filisko, *supra* note 63 at 55 (discussing S.C. civility code).

[85]   *See, e.g.,* Am. Bd. of Trial Advocates, *The ABOTA Code of Professionalism* (2020).

[86]   ABA Model Code of Judicial Conduct R. 2.8(B) (2015) ("A judge shall be patient, dignified, and courteous to litigants, jurors, witnesses, lawyers, court staff, court officials, and others with whom the judge deals in an official capacity, and shall require similar conduct of lawyers, court staff, court officials, and others subject to the judge's direction and control."). *See, e.g.,* Wendy Davis, *Bullying From the Bench: A Wave of High-Profile Bad Behavior Has Put Scrutiny on Judges,* 105 A.B.A. J. 46 (Mar. 2019).

[87]   Marvin E. Aspen, *supra* note 52 at 96.

[88]   Laura Castro Trognitz, *Bench Talk,* 86 A.B.A. J. 56 (Mar. 2000) (quoting Judge John G. Koeltl of the U.S. Dist. Ct., S.D.N.Y.).

[89]   Douglas S. Lavine, *Advocacy From the Human Perspective: Advice for Young Appellate Lawyers,* 15 J. App. Practice and Process 243, 251 (2014).

[90]   Cliff Sain, *Earth's Atmosphere,* Springfield (Mo.) News-Leader, Feb. 26, 2008, at C3 (quoting President Roosevelt).

[91]   Alfred, Lord Tennyson, *Idylls of the King: The Last Tournament,* line 631 (1859–85).

[92]   Arthur T. Vanderbilt, *Forensic Persuasion,* 7 Wash. & Lee L. Rev. 123, 130 (1950).

[93]   *Id.*

[94]   Louis H. Pollak, *supra* note 50 at 66 (quoting Justice Kennedy).

[95]   ABA Model Rules of Prof'l Conduct, Preamble [1] (2019).

[96]   ABA Model Code of Judicial Conduct, Preamble [1] (2019).

[97]   Laurel Currie Oates & Anne Enquist, The Legal Writing Handbook 583–86 (5th ed. 2010).

[98]   Ken Schwartz, *Obama Signs Law "Modernizing" Federal References to Minorities,* Voice of Am. News (May 23, 2016).

[99]   H.R. 4238, P.L. 114–157 (signed into law May 20, 2016).

[100]   *E.g.,* 1 U.S.C. § 1 (2019) ("In determining the meaning of any Act of Congress, unless the context indicates otherwise—... words importing the masculine gender include the feminine as well"); Mo. Rev. Stat. § 1.030 (2019) ("When any subject matter, party or person is described or referred to by words importing ... the masculine gender, ... females as well as males ... are included.").

[101] *See, e.g.,* Richard C. Wydick, *supra* note 7 at 74–75; Laurel Currie Oates & Anne Enquist, *supra* note 99 at 578–82; Edward D. Re & Joseph R. Re, Brief Writing & Oral Argument 8–9 (9th ed. 2005); Gerald Lebovits, *He Said-She Said: Gender-Neutral Writing*, 74 N.Y. St. B.J. 64 (Feb. 2002).

[102] *E.g.,* Bill Walsh, *The Post Drops the "Mike"—and the Hyphen in "E-Mail"*, Wash. Post, Dec. 4, 2015 (Wash. Post Style Guide); Benjamin Dreyer, Dreyer's English: An Utterly Correct Guide to Clarity and Style 93 (2019).

PART 2

RESEARCHING

■ ■ ■

Legal writing depends on thorough research into fact and law. Thoroughness may begin with consulting the client and others for background and context. Thoroughness also means synthesizing case law, statutory codes, administrative regulations, legal commentary, and other relevant official and unofficial sources.

Ineffective research usually begets ineffective writing. Ineffectiveness on both counts likely determined the outcome in *Lochner v. New York* (1905), the constitutional landmark chronicled in Chapter 3.[1] The state attorney general's Supreme Court brief demonstrated both overconfidence and apparent lack of professional commitment to robust advocacy. The outcome was what Chief Justice William H. Rehnquist later called "one of the most ill-starred decisions" that the Court has ever handed down.[2]

The Court's decision in *Kennedy v. Louisiana* (2008),[3] chronicled in Chapter 4, shows how judicial decision making can suffer when research by committed advocates overlooks a relevant source. Oversights happen, but thoroughness remains the goal.

Quite apart from the two decisions' holdings and rationales, the decisions hold enduring lessons relevant to the primacy of research in legal writing. Chapters 3 and 4 introduce these lessons.

---

[1]   198 U.S. 45 (1905).

[2]   William H. Rehnquist, The Supreme Court: How It Was, How It Is 205 (1987).

[3]   554 U.S. 407, *reh'g denied*, 554 U.S. 945 (2008).

CHAPTER 3

DID BAD BRIEFING DECIDE
LOCHNER V. NEW YORK?

■ ■ ■

On Thursday morning, February 23, 1905, Chief Justice Melville W. Fuller opened oral argument in *Lochner v. New York*, a nondescript case that attracted little press notice.[1] More than a century later, the Supreme Court's decision remains a staple of law school constitutional law classes because the holding triggered social and political forces that changed the course of American constitutional history. According to one commentator, *Lochner* "continues to hover over constitutional law like a ghost."[2]

In 1902, New York State fined rural bakery owner Joseph Lochner $50 for employing a worker for more than 60 hours a week in violation of the state's Bakeshop Act. The Act's enactors had unanimously found that toiling longer hours—as many as 12 or more a day for six to seven days a week—in damp, dusty, rat-infested bakeries in slum tenement cellars debilitated most workers before they turned 45 and caused many to die young.[3]

Over sharp dissents by Justices Oliver Wendell Holmes and John Marshall Harlan, the Supreme Court overturned the bakery owner's misdemeanor conviction. The Court held, 5–4, that the Bakeshop Act violated "liberty of contract," an interest that a few Court decisions had found in the Fourteenth Amendment's Due Process Clause.

The constitutional liberty enjoyed by Joseph Lochner and his employees to negotiate terms of employment, wrote Justice Rufus W. Peckham for the slim majority, turned on a core issue. Was the Bakeshop Act "a fair, reasonable and appropriate exercise of the police power of the State"?[4] Or was the Act "an unreasonable, unnecessary, and arbitrary interference with the right of the individual to his personal liberty or to enter into those contracts in relation to labor which may seem to him appropriate and necessary for the support of himself and his family"?[5]

The final word on *Lochner's* antagonistic substantive due process touchstones—reasonableness or arbitrariness—lay not with the political branches, but with courts that grew increasingly hostile to federal and state economic regulation. By the time the nation confronted the Depression in the early 1930s, the decision had morphed into what two historians call a "constitutional monstrosity" that "disembowel[ed] federal and state efforts to protect workers from predatory employers."[6]

The Supreme Court interred *Lochner's* economic substantive due process doctrine in 1937, but not before striking down nearly 200 social welfare and economic regulatory measures.[7] *Lochner's* demise led to Justice Harlan Fiske Stone's Footnote Four in *United States v. Carolene Products Co.* (1938).[8] The footnote foreshadowed today's tiered constitutional analysis by distinguishing the Court's new deference to economic regulation from heightened scrutiny of challenges that implicate cherished personal liberties and civil rights.

AN INCIPIENT "BRANDEIS BRIEF"

The significance of *Lochner's* economic substantive due process doctrine spotlights the unlikely choices of two swing Justices—Henry Billings Brown and Joseph McKenna—to join what became the bare 5–4 victory for defendant Joseph Lochner. During the Court's deliberations, were the two influenced to change their votes by the defendant's sterling, well-researched brief, which outshined the paltry, poorly researched brief filed by the New York Attorney General? The stark imbalance in briefing presents one of the compelling "what ifs" of American constitutional history because a decision for the state would have paved alternative doctrinal pathways to destinations unknown.

Labor leader Samuel Gompers speculated later that the Supreme Court might have held for the State if the Justices could have seen for themselves the squalid working conditions in many of the nation's bakeries, including Joseph Lochner's.[9] With the Court unable to take testimony from eyewitnesses or experts, however, the parties' briefs were the Justices' eyes and ears as they proceeded to decision. In a case that turned on the Court's perceptions of reasonableness or arbitrariness, Joseph Lochner's defense counsel out-briefed New York's Attorney General.

To establish that New York's maximum hours law was an unreasonable exercise of the state's police power, defense counsel submitted a lengthy, well-documented brief whose appendix supplemented legal doctrine with studies from medical journals indicating that bakery work was not inherently hazardous to employees' health.[10] One scholar has called the submission "an incipient 'Brandeis Brief.' "[11] The term "Brandeis Brief" today describes a filing that combines legal analysis with relevant evidence from the social sciences or other non-legal disciplines. But lawyer Louis D. Brandeis did not prevail with his fabled Supreme Court brief until *Muller v. Oregon*,[12] which distinguished *Lochner* in 1908, three years after the New York bakery owner's brief helped set an example.

NINETEEN PAGES THAT CHANGED HISTORY

The New York Attorney General's office evidently did not take Joseph Lochner's Supreme Court appeal seriously, a costly lapse that seems particularly surprising because the state's two appellate courts had each affirmed the conviction by one-vote margins over strong dissents.[13] The office's meager 19-page brief presented little factual analysis or legal argument, cited few precedents, and barely mentioned available medical authorities that described serious health hazards and frequent early death from overwork in dank bakeries.[14] The Attorney General squandered an opportunity to persuade the Justices because his office did not even try to expand on medical discussion advanced by a concurring judge when the New York Court of Appeals, the state's highest court, upheld Joseph Lochner's conviction.[15]

Historians have speculated about why the Attorney General's office devoted only halfhearted research to Lochner's Supreme Court appeal. Three plausible explanations teach how not to approach research in written advocacy.

First, the Attorney General may have assumed a relatively easy victory because, in *Holden v. Hardy* only seven years earlier, the Court had upheld Utah's maximum hours statute for coal miners by a seemingly comfortable 7-to-2 margin.[16] Even if not overconfident, Attorney General Julius M. Mayer may have lacked personal and professional commitment for the challenged Bakeshop Act because he opposed most economic regulatory legislation.[17] Or perhaps he and his staff brushed aside Joseph Lochner's case because his office faced pressing deadlines in another Supreme Court appeal that seemed more important, though the other appeal's decision would pass into history unremembered.[18]

THE COURT'S DELIBERATIONS IN *LOCHNER*

Whatever the explanations for the New York Attorney General's lukewarm effort in *Lochner*, the imbalance in the parties' briefing may have turned a razor-thin victory for the State into a razor-thin victory for the bakery owner. Justice Brown had written the majority opinion upholding maximum-hours legislation in *Holden v. Hardy*, and neither he nor Justice McKenna had ever voted to strike down state labor legislation for violating the Fourteenth Amendment.[19] Evidence indicates that Justice Harlan initially drafted the majority opinion in *Lochner*, and that Justice Peckham initially drafted a dissent. Justice Harlan's son said later that his father's original *Lochner* draft was for the majority, and a commentator argues that the tone and structure of Justice Harlan's ultimate dissent suggest the switch.[20]

On April 17, *Lochner's* slim five-Justice majority—with Justices Brown and McKenna safely on board—struck down New York's Bakeshop

Act as unreasonable, unnecessary, and arbitrary. The majority concluded that the Act had "no . . . direct relation to, and no . . . substantial effect upon, the health of the employee."[21]

The Court chose a path that led to judicial encroachment on the roles of the political branches, and ultimately to a reaction that produced the *Carolene Products* footnote and the later redefinition of constitutional analysis. The reaction has outlived *Lochner's* official demise because, in the 21st century, dissenting Justices still sometimes cite the 1905 decision to charge the majority with abandoning judicial restraint.[22]

LOCHNER'S INSTRUCTIONS
FOR LEGAL RESEARCH

Even for today's advocates who never brief an appeal as ultimately profound as *Lochner*, the two swing Justices' apparent changes of heart underscore the role of lawyers' personal and professional commitment, which Chapter 2 discussed. The New York Attorney General's office overlooked or ignored sources that could have turned the case, and the State paid the price for tepid factual and legal research and writing.

Lochner's evident turnabout from a victory for the State to a victory for the convicted defendant also demonstrates that no case is "easy" until after entry of final judgment and exhaustion of the appellate process. Overconfidence can prove costly in any competition, and litigation remains a competition between adversaries who each pursue victory.

Finally, personal indifference and law office constraints remain poor excuses for lackluster researching or ineffective writing. Once the lawyer undertakes representation in the exercise of professional responsibility, the lawyer's personal feelings no longer count because the client comes first.

---

[1]   198 U.S. 45 (1905). Chapters 3 and 4 are adapted from Douglas E. Abrams, Lochner v. New York *(1905) and* Kennedy v. Louisiana *(2008): Judicial Reliance on Adversary Argument*, 39 Hastings Const. L. Q. 179 (2011).

[2]   Gary D. Rowe, Lochner *Revisionism Revisited*, 24 Law & Soc. Inquiry 221, 222–23 (1999).

[3]   Paul Kens, Lochner v. New York: Economic Regulation on Trial 6–14 (1998).

[4]   198 U.S. at 56.

[5]   *Id.*

[6]   Harold M. Hyman & William M. Wiecek, Equal Justice Under Law: Constitutional Development 1835–1875, at 480 (1982).

[7]   Obergefell v. Hodges, 576 U.S. 644, 135 S. Ct. 2584, 2617 (2015) (Roberts, C.J., dissenting).

[8]   United States v. Carolene Products Co., 304 U.S. 144, 152 n.4 (1938).

[9]   Paul Kens, *supra* note 3 at 35.

[10]   David E. Bernstein, Lochner v. New York: *A Centennial Retrospective*, 83 Wash. U. L.Q. 1469, 1494–96 (2005).

[11]   Stephen A. Siegel, Lochner *Era Jurisprudence and the American Constitutional Tradition*, 70 N.C. L. Rev. 1, 19 n.77 (1991).

[12]   208 U.S. 412 (1908).

[13]   People v. Lochner, 76 N.Y.S. 396 (App. Div. 1902) (3–2 vote), *aff'd*, 69 N.E. 373 (N.Y. 1904) (4–3 vote), *rev'd*, Lochner v. New York, 198 U.S. 45 (1905).

[14]   Paul Kens, *supra* note 3 at 6–14 (1998); David E. Bernstein, *supra* note 10, at 1494–96.

[15]   People v. Lochner, 69 N.E. 373, 382–84 (N.Y. 1904) (Vann, J., concurring), *rev'd*, Lochner v. New York, 198 U.S. 45 (1905).

[16]   169 U.S. 366 (1898); David E. Bernstein, *The Story of* Lochner v. New York: *Impediment to the Growth of the Regulatory State*, in Constitutional Law Stories 299, 317 (Michael C. Dorf ed., 2d ed. 2009).

[17]   Paul Kens, *supra* note 3 at 127.

[18]   *Id.* at 128; David E. Bernstein, *supra* note 10 at 1494–96.

[19]   David E. Bernstein, *supra* note 16 at 317.

[20]   *Id.* at 317 & n.109.

[21]   Lochner, 198 U.S. at 64.

[22]   *See, e.g.*, Obergefell, *supra* note 7 at 135 S. Ct. 2621–23 (Roberts, C.J., dissenting).

CHAPTER 4

THE LEGISLATION EVERYONE MISSED IN
KENNEDY V. LOUISIANA

■ ■ ■

The central role of research in legal writing, so evident in *Lochner*, assumed the spotlight when the Supreme Court decided *Kennedy v. Louisiana* in 2008.[1] *Kennedy* held, 5–4, that the Eighth Amendment prohibits imposition of the death penalty for rape of a child where the crime did not result, and was not intended to result, in the victim's death. No Justice cited a relevant two-year-old congressional enactment that the parties' briefing overlooked, and that neither the Justice Department nor any *amicus curiae* (friend of the court) brief brought to the Court's attention.

"A SPECTACLE OF SOUND AND FURY"

Kennedy's Eighth Amendment holding depended on whether capital punishment for non-fatal rape of a child was consistent with "the evolving standards of decency that mark the progress of a maturing society."[2] Writing for the majority, Justice Anthony M. Kennedy concluded that "[t]he evidence of a national consensus with respect to the death penalty for child rapists ... shows divided opinion but, on balance, an opinion against it."[3] The Court stated that a rapist of a child could be executed in only six of the 36 states that authorize capital punishment, and could not be executed under federal law.[4]

The dissent by Justice Samuel A. Alito, Jr. (joined by Chief Justice John G. Roberts, Jr. and Justices Antonin Scalia and Clarence Thomas) challenged the majority's finding of a national consensus.[5] The dissenters disputed the lineup of the states and its meaning, but they took no issue with the majority's statement that federal law did not permit capital punishment for rape of a child.

Two days after the Court handed down *Kennedy*, a military law blogger reported that the nine Justices had overlooked a recent authority.[6] Ten briefs were filed in the case, but neither party and no *amicus* informed the Court that in a 421-page omnibus military authorization bill in 2006, Congress included a half-page provision that amended the Uniform Code of Military Justice to add the death penalty for rape of a child.[7] The omnibus bill passed overwhelmingly, 95–0 in the Senate and 374–41 in the

House.[8] Nor did any brief in *Kennedy* inform the Court that President George W. Bush signed the legislation and implemented the provision with an executive order that added the death penalty to the Manual for Courts-Martial.[9]

News of the *Kennedy* oversight spread quickly from coast to coast when a front-page *New York Times* story reported it.[10] The White House press secretary told reporters that the Administration was "disturbed . . . that the Court's decision might be based on a mistake."[11] Eighty-five Congress members signed a letter asking the Justices to rehear the case because "a central factual basis for the majority opinion was not only incomplete, but inaccurate."[12] The *Washington Post* urged the Court to grant rehearing because "[t]he Supreme Court's legitimacy depends not only on the substance of its rulings but also on the quality of its deliberations."[13]

The Solicitor General did not file a brief in *Kennedy*, but the Justice Department expressed regret that it had overlooked the 2006 congressional enactment. The parties missed the enactment, but the Department acknowledged its responsibility to inform the Court about federal law.[14]

The state of Louisiana admitted that the 2006 congressional enactment "eluded everyone's research."[15] Defense counsel said that his research revealed only an older military capital punishment provision that "[w]e just assumed . . . was defunct. We figured if somebody in the government thought otherwise, we'd hear about it."[16]

Louisiana's petition for rehearing argued that the State's "significant error . . . should neither inhibit the Court's work nor diminish its fealty to the Constitution."[17] "[B]oth political branches," the petition urged, "have recently and affirmatively authorized the death penalty for child rape. . . . Such a clear expression of democratic will, at the very least, calls into question the conclusion that there is a 'national consensus against' the practice."[18]

In its *amicus* brief supporting the State's petition for rehearing, the Justice Department argued that the Court's "erroneous and materially incomplete assessment of the 'national consensus' concerning capital punishment for child rape . . . undermines the foundation for the Court's decision."[19] "[R]ehearing is warranted," the Department concluded, "to ensure that a material omission in the decisionmaking process has not tainted the Court's decision on a matter of such profound constitutional, moral, and practical importance."[20]

The Court aroused what the *Christian Science Monitor* called "a spectacle of sound and fury"[21] when it denied rehearing on the first day of its new term but added footnotes and a few words to the majority and dissenting opinions before they reached the United States Reports.[22] Writing for the five-Justice majority that denied rehearing, Justice Kennedy explained that congressional authorization of the death penalty for non-fatal child rape in the military "does not draw into question our conclusions that there is a consensus against the death penalty for the crime in the civilian context."[23]

The *Washington Post* warned that "the court may have damaged, even if slightly, its own reputation" by "leav[ing]—deservedly or not—the impression that a majority of the court refused to hear new facts and alter their positions."[24]

KENNEDY'S INSTRUCTIONS FOR LEGAL RESEARCH

Judicial reliance on adversary briefing, evident in *Lochner* and *Kennedy*, remains a cornerstone of the nation's civil and criminal justice systems. No Justice deciding *Kennedy* had a military law background that would have encouraged personal awareness or discovery of a death penalty provision in a recent omnibus military appropriations bill that numbered more than 400 pages.

Neither the media nor any commentator suggested that the oversight in *Kennedy's* briefs arose from lack of personal and professional commitment similar to that which likely characterized the New York Attorney General's indifferent performance in *Lochner*. But recognition that advocates' research might sometimes miss relevant authorities or issues is nearly as old as the American judicial system itself. The Supreme Court has long held that "[q]uestions which merely lurk in the record, neither brought to the attention of the court nor ruled upon, are not to be considered as having been so decided as to constitute precedents."[25] This holding, a safety valve designed at least partly to enable courts to deny precedential effect to a matter previously missed, dates from an opinion that Chief Justice John Marshall delivered for the Court in 1805.[26]

The Court's public misstep in *Kennedy* reinforces the value of meticulous research, free from a party's assumptions or tacit reliance on adversaries or *amici*. In federal or state courts at any level, judges and their law clerks sometimes pursue independent research when an evident shortcoming appears in the parties' submissions, but this pursuit remains the exception rather than the rule. The shortcoming may not be readily apparent, and independent judicial research imposes institutional costs on courts that manage swollen dockets. Independent judicial research may also create friction with the adversary system, which (unlike the inquisitorial system that prevails in most of Europe) charges litigants and not the court with advancing the factual and legal predicates for decision making.[27]

Five months before he ascended to the Supreme Court bench in 1916, private lawyer Louis D. Brandeis identified judicial reliance on adversary research and briefing as foundations of decision making: "[A] judge rarely performs his functions adequately unless the case before him is adequately presented."[28] The Justices decided *Lochner* and *Kennedy* with authorities that counsel's research provided them, a circumstance that recalls the instruction of then-Judge Oliver Wendell Holmes in 1885: "The law is made by the Bar, even more than by the Bench."[29]

---

[1]   554 U.S. 407, *reh'g denied*, 554 U.S. 945 (2008). Chapters 3 and 4 are adapted from Douglas E. Abrams, Lochner v. New York *(1905) and* Kennedy v. Louisiana *(2008): Judicial Reliance on Adversary Argument*, 39 Hastings Const. L. Q. 179 (2011).

[2]   554 U.S. at 419.

[3]   *Id.* at 426.

[4]   *Id.* at 422–26.

[5]   *Id.* at 448–61 (Alito, J., dissenting).

[6]   Dwight Sullivan, *The Supremes Dis the Military Justice System* (June 28, 2008), http://caaflog.blogspot.com/2008/06/supremes-dis-military-justice-system.html (visited Aug. 14, 2020).

[7]   *Nat'l Defense Authorization Act for Fiscal Year 2006*, Pub. L. No. 109–163, 119 Stat. 3136, 3264, § 553(a) (2006); 10 U.S.C. §§ 856, 920 (2000 ed., and Supp. V).

[8]   *Roll call vote for H.R. 1815, 109th Cong.* (Dec. 19, 2005) https://www.congress.gov/bill/109th-congress/house-bill/1815 (visited Aug. 15, 2020).

[9]   *Executive Order No. 13,447*, 72 Fed. Reg. 56179 (Sept. 28, 2007); Manual for Courts-Martial, United States, Part IV, Art. 120, P 45.f(1), p. IV–78 (2008).

[10]   Linda Greenhouse, *In Court Ruling on Executions, a Factual Flaw*, N.Y. Times, July 2, 2008, at 1.

[11]   Linda Greenhouse, *Justice Dept. Admits Error In Failure to Brief Court*, N.Y. Times, July 3, 2008, at 15.

[12]   Douglas E. Abrams, Lochner v. New York *(1905) and* Kennedy v. Louisiana *(2008): Judicial Reliance on Adversary Argument*, 39 Hastings Const. L. Q. 179, 186 n.43 (2011).

[13]   *Supreme Slip-Up*, Wash. Post, July 5, 2008, at 6 (editorial).

[14]   Linda Greenhouse, *supra* note 11 at 15.

[15]   Linda Greenhouse, *supra* note 10 at 1.

[16]   *Id.*

[17]   Petition for reh'g at 3, Kennedy v. Louisiana, 554 U.S. 407 (2008) (No. 07–343), 2008 WL 2847069.

[18]   *Id.*

[19]   Mot. for Leave to File Br. and Br. for the United States as Amicus Curiae Supp. Pet. for Reh'g at 2, Kennedy v. Louisiana (July 2008), in Douglas E. Abrams, *supra* note 12 at 188 note 54.

[20]   *Id.*

[21]   Warren Richey, *Despite Gaffe, Supreme Court Won't Revisit Landmark Child-Rape Ruling*, Christian Sci. Mon., Oct. 2, 2008, at 25.

[22]   Kennedy v. Louisiana, 554 U.S. at 426 n.*, 459 n.6 (Alito, J., dissenting).

[23]   *Id.* at 948 (statement of Kennedy, J., denying rehearing).

[24]   *Case Closed*, Wash. Post, Oct. 2, 2008, at A22 (editorial).

[25]   Webster v. Fall, 266 U.S. 507, 511 (1925).

[26]   United States v. More, 7 U.S. (3 Cranch) 159, 172 (1805) ("No question was made, in that case, as to the jurisdiction. It passed *sub silentio*, and the court does not consider itself as bound by that case.").

[27]   *E.g.,* Douglas E. Abrams, *supra* note 12 at 189.

[28]   Louis D. Brandeis, *The Living Law*, 10 Ill. L. Rev. 461, 470 (1916).

[29]   Oliver Wendell Holmes, *The Law* (Feb. 5, 1885), in Speeches by Oliver Wendell Holmes 16, 16 (1934).

PART 3

WRITING

■ ■ ■

Chapter 2's basic strategies begin the writing process. Research proceeds, and the lawyer begins committing words to the page. Chapter 5 presents the four fundamentals of good legal writing—conciseness, precision, simplicity, and clarity.

These fundamentals, and other rules such as the conventions of grammar and syntax, deserve adherence most of the time because they enhance content, meaning, and style most of the time. But Chapter 6 explores a Rule of Reason that encourages purposeful departures from the rules to sharpen the writer's message.

Rules and purposeful departures do not end the story. The adversary system depends on lawyers whose persuasive writing is marked not only by fidelity to the fundamentals, but also by vigorous expression that combines reason and passion, two rhetorical forces that Chapter 7 explores.

CHAPTER 5

THE FOUR FUNDAMENTALS OF GOOD WRITING

■ ■ ■

Poet, writer, Librarian of Congress, three-time Pulitzer Prize winner, and Massachusetts Bar member Archibald MacLeish had a message for legal writers. "[L]awyers would be better off if they stopped thinking of the language of the law as a different language and realized that the art of writing for legal purposes is in no way distinguishable from the art of writing for any other purpose."[1]

Recall from Chapter 2 that the English language knows only two types of writing—good writing and bad writing. This core proposition means that lawyers can learn valuable lessons from accomplished literary figures and other prominent writers, most of whom (unlike MacLeish) had no training in the law. Lessons from some of these voices have already appeared in earlier chapters. This chapter recites additional perspectives that these voices have bequeathed about good writing.

Like most analogies, ones that link literature and legal writing remain imperfect at their edges. "Literature is not the goal of lawyers, though they occasionally attain it," wrote Professor Felix Frankfurter eight years before he joined the Supreme Court.[2] "The law," Justice Oliver Wendell Holmes said earlier, "is not the place for the artist or the poet."[3]

Despite some imperfections in literature-and-legal-writing analogies, insights from prominent fiction and non-fiction writers can serve lawyers well because good writing of any genre stems from what Pulitzer Prize-winning historian Barbara W. Tuchman calls "that magnificent instrument that lies at the command of all of us—the English language."[4]

The tone and cadence of non-lawyer writers may vary sometimes from those of professionals who write in the law, but the core aim remains communication enhanced by Professor Weihofen's quartet—conciseness, precision, simplicity, and clarity.

CONCISENESS

"I write as straight as I can, just as I walk as straight as
I can, because that is the best way to get there."

—H.G. Wells[5]

Luminaries identify the essence of conciseness. "Brevity is the soul of wit," wrote William Shakespeare in *Hamlet*.[6] "Less is more," agreed British Victorian poet and playwright Robert Browning, wasting no words.[7] "It is with words as with sunbeams. The more condensed, the deeper they burn," explained British Romantic poet Robert Southey.[8] "Brevity and simplicity," wrote British historian and educator Thomas Arnold, are "two of the greatest merits which style can have."[9]

"Great is the art of beginning, but greater the art is of ending."

—Henry Wadsworth Longfellow[10]

Conciseness means paring the written document's overall length to the extent possible without sacrificing content. If a lawyer can effectively convey the message in five pages, consuming ten risks losing audience members before the finish. Readers with a choice may feel tempted not even to start, and weary readers may stop before the end. When a writing's overall length intimidates, skimming or turning away entirely may seem the easier alternative. Readers may turn away before the end because they find the content unappealing or unsuited to their needs, but readers may also turn away once they sense that the writing appears too long for the message it seeks to convey.

Opera singer Dorothy Sarnoff offered a simple formula for success on stage: "Make sure you have finished speaking before your audience has finished listening."[11] Effective writing depends on a similar formula—make sure you have finished writing before your readers have finished reading. The formula remains central because, as Admiral James Stavridis noted in 2019, readers' "[a]ttention spans have spiraled resolutely downward" in recent years.[12]

"This report, by its very length, defends itself
against the risk of being read."

—Sir Winston Churchill[13]

Amid the personal and professional distractions that mark what journalist Bill Moyers calls the "seductions and demands of modern life,"[14] conciseness helps writers hold readers' attention until the end. When clients' rights and obligations hang in the balance, lawyers may have no choice but to plod through unwieldy adversary briefs or motion papers, overwritten judicial opinions, or unnecessarily verbose legislation or administrative regulations. But even with such an essentially captive audience, overwriting risks camouflaging the truly important points.

British poet Alexander Pope likely never opened a law text, but he warned that "[w]ords are like leaves; and where they most abound, much fruit of sense beneath is rarely found."[15]

Leading advocates and judges have recognized the value of conciseness. Legendary Supreme Court advocate John W. Davis, for example, said that the most effective briefs are "models of brevity."[16] He exalted the "courage of exclusion"[17] because the court "may read as much or as little as it chooses."[18]

"I have yet to put down a brief," reports Chief Justice Roberts, "and say, 'I wish that had been longer.' . . . Almost every brief I've read could be shorter."[19] Justice Benjamin N. Cardozo warned earlier that "[a]nalysis is useless if it destroys what it is intended to explain."[20] Justice Robert H. Jackson advised advocates that "[l]egal contentions, like the currency, depreciate through over-issue."[21]

In many jurisdictions, lower-court dockets have increased faster than population in recent decades, reportedly diminishing many judges' patience with overwritten submissions. After 19 years on the D.C. Circuit federal bench, Judge Patricia M. Wald shared candid advice with advocates: "The more paper you throw at us, the meaner we get, the more irritated and hostile we feel about verbosity, peripheral arguments and long footnotes."[22]

"Many judges look first to see how long a document is before reading a word," Judge Wald confided. "If it is long, they automatically read fast; if short, they read slower. Figure out yourself which is better for your case."[23]

Lawyers and judges alike can appreciate this short verse by Dr. Seuss (Theodor Geisel), who wrote for children, but often with an eye toward adults: "[T]he writer who breeds/ more words than he needs/ is making a chore/ for the reader who reads./ That's why my belief is/ the briefer the brief is,/ the greater the sigh/ of the reader's relief is."[24]

"I have made this [letter] longer than usual, only because
I have not had the time to make it shorter."

—*French writer and mathematician Blaise Pascal*[25]

From early drafts onward, managing a writing's overall length demands self-discipline because verbosity can be the path of least resistance, especially now that the personal computer has displaced the pen. Churchill said that "it is sheer laziness not compressing thought into a reasonable space."[26] Admiral Stavridis calls attention to "the clarity that comes from disciplined thought and writing."[27]

"Often it takes longer to write shorter opinions," attests Justice Elena Kagan.[28] Pascal's lament also resonates with any brief writer who has ever struggled to argue within page limits imposed by court rules. A federal district judge acknowledges that "in matters of legal writing brevity is more challenging than prolixity," but the judge also advised that "courts generally are more appreciative of the former than of the latter."[29]

"Many a poem is marred by a superfluous verse."

—Henry Wadsworth Longfellow[30]

Conciseness means not only managing a writing's overall length, but also delivering words and sentences that contribute sinew, not fat. "The most valuable of all talent is that of never using two words when one will do," said lawyer Thomas Jefferson, who found "[n]o stile of writing . . . so delightful as that which is all pith, which never omits a necessary word, nor uses an unnecessary one."[31]

Pith depends on trimming line by line. "A sentence," wrote Strunk and White in *The Elements of Style*, "should contain no unnecessary words, a paragraph no unnecessary sentences, for the same reason that a drawing should have no unnecessary lines and a machine no unnecessary parts."[32]

Roman writer and orator Marcus Tullius Cicero explained that "[e]very word that is unnecessary only pours over the side of a brimming mind."[33] British poet, essayist, and biographer Samuel Johnson likened a writer "who uses a great many words to express his meaning" to "a bad marksman who, instead of aiming a single stone at an object, takes up a handful and throws at it in hopes he may hit."[34]

Concise legal writing is lean and strong, free from distracting verbiage that can clutter and thus weaken the message. Aside from clutter, "[u]nnecessary words increase the opportunities for you and your reader to go wrong."[35] These words can provide ammunition to a reader who seeks ways to distinguish or refashion the writer's argument.

Trimming sentences and words from early drafts remains a primary task of editing by the writer or a third person, the subject of Part Four below. Three questions dominate the editorial process. Does the particular sentence or word sustain the message? Does it detract from the message? Would the message emerge equally strong, or even stronger, with the contemplated trimming?

"[E]ven when you cut, you don't."

—Nobel Peace Prize Laureate Elie Wiesel[36]

When a lawyer carefully trims a document's length and words, the lawyer need not worry about sacrificing paragraphs, sentences, or words to the "delete" key. The writer's thoughts can survive in the tighter narrative. "Writing is not like painting where you add," Wiesel explains. "Writing is more like a sculpture where you remove. . . . There is a difference between a book of two hundred pages from the very beginning, and a book of two hundred pages which is the result of an original eight hundred pages. The six hundred pages are there. Only you don't see them."[37]

"[T]he great thing about a writer's life," adds historian David McCullough, is that "nothing is useless, everything bears on future work."[38] When a writer deletes passages or words today, nothing necessarily goes to waste if the writer saves the deletions in a separate electronic file. If the writer likes the deleted material now, the writer may find a place for it in a future writing.

"How gladly would I exchange my hundred
pages for your twenty lines."[39]

—*Edward Everett to Abraham Lincoln, November 20, 1863*

Little underscores the value of effective writing more graphically than stories rich in Americana. Lawyers can learn much about the virtues of conciseness and brevity from examples set by two legendary role models.

The first role model is Justice Oliver Wendell Holmes, who wrote some of the Supreme Court's most elegant, most forceful—and briefest—opinions. According to an often-told story, Fanny Bowditch Holmes entered her elderly husband's office one day and found him writing while standing erect at a podium. "Nothing conduces to brevity," the Justice explained, "like a caving in of the knees."[40]

Holmes was a 22-year-old lieutenant colonel in the Union army when the second role model, the 19th century's most celebrated country lawyer, helped dedicate a national cemetery to fallen Civil War soldiers on November 19, 1863. The former country lawyer was a late invitee because organizers did not seek much from his attendance. The period has been called America's "golden age of oratory," and the day's main attraction was Edward Everett, the nation's most eminent orator.

Everett held the podium for more than two hours and spoke more than 13,000 words. When he finally sat down, the former country lawyer surprised listeners with a speech that lasted less than two minutes and consisted of fewer than 300 words. No photograph of the former country lawyer's delivery survives because he finished speaking before a photographer had a chance to set up his camera equipment.[41]

The former country lawyer was Abraham Lincoln. The national cemetery was at Gettysburg, Pennsylvania. The speech was the Gettysburg Address, perhaps the most famous speech in American history, one that has remained on schoolchildren's lips for generations. The President had barely any formal education, but years at the bar had taught him how to Know the Audience and how to Earn the Right to a Reader. Mindful that newspapers typically published important speeches in their entirety, and that war-weary readers needed presidential stimulus to persevere, Lincoln delivered a concise message to an audience of readers who included legions beyond the new cemetery's earshot.

Indeed, some of the earliest praise for the Gettysburg Address came from readers who were nowhere near the cemetery on that chilly November day. Essayist Ralph Waldo Emerson later predicted that the President's address "will not easily be surpassed by words on any recorded occasion."[42] "Perhaps [in] no language, ancient or modern, are any number of words found more touching or eloquent," echoed Harriet Beecher Stowe, whose *Uncle Tom's Cabin* also graces the nation's literary heritage.[43]

Everett's sterling career included service as a U.S. Representative, U.S. Senator, Massachusetts Governor, Minister to Great Britain, Secretary of State, and Harvard University professor and president. But his Gettysburg oration left no written word or phrase worth remembering, and he realized immediately that the President had outdone him.

"I should be glad," he wrote Lincoln the next day, "if . . . I came as near to the central idea of the occasion in two hours, as you did in two minutes."[44] "My speech will soon be forgotten; yours never will be."[45] The verdict of history has proved Everett correct on both accounts.

Sometimes "[b]revity becomes of itself a source of obscurity."

—Justice Joseph Story[46]

Justice Joseph Story presented a caveat about concise writing, and he was in solid position to do so because he is the most prolific, versatile legal writer in Supreme Court history. During most of his long tenure on the Court (1811–1845), he also served as the first Dane Professor at Harvard Law School. He became known as the "American Blackstone" because his full-length treatises remained definitive for most of the 19th century. By linking brevity and obscurity, Justice Story recognized that writers should treat conciseness with wary eyes.

Conciseness can help the lawyer finish writing before the readers finish reading, but conciseness is not an end in itself. The lawyer's better approach is "measured brevity," which conveys the message as concisely and efficiently as possible under the circumstances. Where full exposition of fact or law requires extended discussion within limits set by court rules or other standards, a longer presentation may serve the best interests of the client or cause. A few months before he ascended to the Supreme Court bench in 1943, Judge Wiley B. Rutledge advised advocates to strike a balance by being "as brief as one can consistently with adequate and clear presentation of his case."[47]

Knowing the Audience may also play a role because unreasonable brevity may lead some readers to conclude that the writer takes them lightly. The administration of justice demands both actual justice and the appearance of justice; legal writing similarly demands both the writer's seriousness of purpose and the appearance of seriousness. To convey the proper impression, the lawyer sometimes must maintain a writing's length.

PRECISION

"Words are seductive and dangerous material, to be used with caution. . . . [C]areless use of words can leave a false impression one had not intended."

—Historian Barbara W. Tuchman[48]

Words are the lawyer's tools, and perceptive legal writers choose them carefully because they know that readers are unlikely to extend a helping hand. When a writer sends a personal message to a friendly reader, the reader may help by recasting imprecise words in the mind. "I know what my friend really meant to say," the cooperative reader thinks silently. The reader "knows" because the reader wants to know, even if the writer did not quite say it.

In the adversary system of civil and criminal justice, however, readers normally do not throw lawyers such lifelines. Lawyers' writing frequently faces a "hostile audience," one that will "do its best to find the weaknesses in the prose, even perhaps to find ways of turning the words against their intended meaning."[49] Judges and their law clerks, for example, dissect briefs to test arguments, but only after opposing counsel has sought to distinguish arguments troublesome to the opponent.[50]

Lawyers inevitably weaken the client's position when they must beseech adversaries or decision makers to acknowledge what the brief or other filing "really meant to say." Clients and adversaries can lose respect for the lawyer's competence, and decision makers might entertain second thoughts about the strength of the lawyer's arguments.

People do not get a second chance to make a good first impression. Imprecise writing may leave the lawyer no second chance to make any sort of impression because trial courts frequently decide motions on the parties' written filings, without oral argument. Appellate courts have reduced oral argument to a few minutes per side, often largely for give-and-take between court and counsel about matters raised in previously submitted briefs or memoranda. Imprecise writing can derail lawyers and their clients before they ever reach the courtroom, or can compromise the record that will shape an appeal.

This contemporary primacy of written appellate advocacy is a relatively recent development in our nation's legal history. "Early oral advocates were unconstrained by any time limitations," explains Justice Sandra Day O'Connor about the Supreme Court. "When they presented their arguments, they were 'heard in silence for hours, without being stopped or interrupted' by the Justices. . . . [O]ral arguments could last for ten days."[51] In two early landmark cases that remain staples of constitutional law curricula—*McCulloch v. Maryland* (1819) and *Gibbons v. Ogden* (1824)—oral argument lasted nine days and five days respectively.[52]

These vintage clashes make for good history, but they describe a bygone era. When a constitution, statute, or rule confers the right to a "hearing" today, judges and other decision makers normally retain discretion to "hear" through the written word and not the spoken language. The nation's earliest advocates would not recognize the centrality of precise writing in 21st century advocacy.

> *"The words in prose ought to express the*
> *intended meaning, and no more."*
>
> —*Samuel Taylor Coleridge*[53]

Guy de Maupassant, France's greatest short-story writer, had a simple formula about precision similar to Coleridge's. "Whatever you want to say," Maupassant asserted, "there is only one word to express it, only one verb to give it movement, only one adjective to qualify it. You must search for that word, that verb, that adjective, and never be content with an approximation, never resort to tricks, even clever ones, and never have recourse to verbal sleight-of-hand to avoid a difficulty."[54]

Coleridge and Maupassant set the bar high, perhaps too high for legal writers. "Anything that is written may present a problem of meaning," Justice Frankfurter explained, because words "seldom attain[ ] more than approximate precision."[55] Former U.S. Attorney General Edward H. Levi similarly understood "the ambiguities of words," which he found "inevitable in both statute and constitution."[56]

Despite this inevitability, President (and later Chief Justice) William Howard Taft challenged lawyers: "Don't write so that you can be understood; write so that you can't be misunderstood."[57] Legal writers may not be able to prevent readers from attempting to refashion a precedent or written argument, but legal writers mindful of precision can make any attempts more difficult.

Achieving the greatest possible precision demands careful preparation, meticulous writing, and close editing. "To get the right word in the right place is a rare achievement," said Mark Twain, whom novelist William Dean Howells once called "sole, incomparable, the Lincoln of our literature."[58]

SIMPLICITY

*"[B]eauty of style and harmony and grace and good
rhythm depend on simplicity."*

—Plato[59]

For legally trained and lay readers alike, law and public policy can be complex enough as it is. Lawyers can serve their clients and causes most effectively with the simplest words that, in the factual and legal context as the lawyer sees it, convey the intended message. Perceptive trial lawyers typically speak short words when they address judges, jurors, or other decision makers in courtrooms or other halls of justice. These trial lawyers seek to preserve force and accuracy, to avoid condescension, and to spurn avoidable complexity that can impede communication about facts or law. Lawyers should pursue similar goals when they commit words to writing.

"If men would only say what they have to say in plain terms," wrote Coleridge, "how much more eloquent they would be!"[60] "[T]o be simple is to be great," agreed essayist and poet Ralph Waldo Emerson, whose writing demonstrated both simplicity and greatness.[61]

Thomas Jefferson left no doubt about where he stood. "I dislike the verbose and intricate style of the English statutes," the elderly lawyer wrote a friend in 1817, "and in our [Virginia's] revised code I endeavored to restore it to the simple [style] of the ancient statutes."[62]

"If you can't explain something simply, you don't understand it well."

—attributed to Albert Einstein[63]

"Make everything as simple as possible, but no simpler."

—paraphrasing Albert Einstein[64]

Commentators sometimes scoff at calls for simplicity in legal writing, reasoning that complex law necessarily begets complex expression. In more than 300 scientific and 150 non-scientific papers, however, Einstein sought to explain complex ideas as simply as possible. "Any fool," he said, "can make things bigger, more complex, and more violent. It takes a touch of genius—and a lot of courage—to move in the opposite direction."[65]

Genius and courage also worked well for Nobel Laureate Paul A. Samuelson, whose classic economics textbooks reached generations of college students by "presenting the issues as simply as we can, but not misleading you with oversimplifications." Samuelson's default position? "Abstract thoughts need plain examples."[66]

The quest for simplicity remains a judgment call dependent on the circumstances as the writer perceives them. On the one hand, simplicity for its own sake (like conciseness for its own sake, discussed above through Justice Story) can impede rather than enhance communication.

On the other hand, legal doctrine and factual argument are often not as complex as they first seem, and reasonable simplicity may lie within the grasp of lawyers who know their audience and strive to Earn the Right to a Reader. "Out of intense complexities," Sir Winston Churchill explained, "intense simplicities emerge."[67]

"One of the really bad things you can do to your writing is to dress up the vocabulary, looking for long words because you're maybe a little bit ashamed of your short ones."

—Stephen King[68]

Ernest Hemingway once heard that William Faulkner had criticized him as someone who "had no courage, never been known to use a word that might send the reader to the dictionary."[69] "Poor Faulkner," Hemingway responded. "Does he really think big emotions come from big words? He thinks I don't know the ten-dollar words. I know them all right. But there are older and simpler and better words, and those are the ones I use."[70]

Simplicity proceeds from overall style to individual word choice. Why say "utilize," for example, when the verb "use" conveys meaning as well or better? In his *Dictionary of Modern English Usage*, H.W. Fowler explained that "shortness is a merit in words" because "short words are not only handier to use, but more powerful in effect; extra syllables reduce, not increase, vigour."[71] "Those who run to long words," Fowler added, "confuse pomposity with dignity, flaccidity with ease, and bulk with force."[72]

"The finest language is mostly made up of simple unimposing words," said British Victorian novelist George Eliot (Mary Ann Evans).[73] In a letter to a 12-year-old boy, Mark Twain praised the youngster for "us[ing] plain, simple language, short words, and brief sentences. That is the way to write English—it is the modern way and the best way. Stick to it; don't let fluff and flowers and verbosity creep in."[74]

Two historical vignettes demonstrate the power of expression in simple, unimposing words.

"Ask not. . . ."

At his inauguration on January 20, 1961, President John F. Kennedy delivered a ringing appeal to national vitality: "And so, my fellow Americans: ask not what your country can do for you—ask what you can do for your country."

Kennedy's charisma enhanced the oral delivery on the U.S. Capitol's East Portico on that frigid day, but the timeless appeal's endurance on the printed page owes much to its simplicity. The President used short words, mostly one-syllable ones, with a few of two syllables. The only word longer than two syllables was "Americans." Would JFK's clarion call still ring today if the new President had said, "*Inquire* not what your country can *accomplish* for you—*inquire* what you can *accomplish* for your country."?

"Trees"

Joyce Kilmer wrote his much-loved poem "Trees" in 1913, five years before a sniper killed him at the Second Battle of the Marne a few months before the end of World War I:

> I think that I shall never see
> A poem lovely as a tree.
>
> A tree whose hungry mouth is prest
> Against the earth's sweet flowing breast;
>
> A tree that looks at God all day,
> And lifts her leafy arms to pray;
>
> A tree that may in summer wear
> A nest of robins in her hair;
>
> Upon whose bosom snow has lain;
> Who intimately lives with rain.
>
> Poems are made by fools like me,
> But only God can make a tree.

As President Kennedy did at his Inaugural, Joyce Kilmer followed a time-tested formula. "Trees" delivered none of the "fluff and flowers and verbosity" that Mark Twain had disparaged in his letter to the young boy. Kilmer wrote short words—nearly all one-syllable, a few two-syllables, and only one longer. More than a century later, the poem still resonates in the popular consciousness.

CLARITY

"Think like a wise man, but communicate in the language of the people."

—*William Butler Yeats*[75]

As an adjunct instructor more than 35 years ago, I began my teaching career with the 1L Legal Research and Writing course. In one of the early lessons, I urged the class to write so that an intelligent high school senior could understand, paying special attention to terms of art that high schoolers (and most non-lawyer adults, and even some lawyers) could not readily grasp without explanation.

Writing for an imaginary intelligent high school audience does not mean insulting professional readers, nor does it mean sacrificing style or content. But it does mean that legal writers who would reach an intelligent high school audience will reach almost any other audience they target. The advice has worked well in my own writing ever since.

*"The chief virtue that language can have is clearness, and
nothing detracts from it so much as the
use of unfamiliar words."*

—Hippocrates[76]

Clarity reaps rewards. "[T]he first end of a writer," British Poet Laureate and literary critic John Dryden counseled in 1700, is "to be understood."[77] "The power of clear statement is the great power at the bar," said Daniel Webster, one of America's greatest advocates.[78]

Clarity remains a virtue on both sides of the bench. Justice Robert H. Jackson stressed the Supreme Court's responsibility "to do our utmost to make clear and understandable the reasons for deciding cases as we do."[79] At the end of the 20th century, Chief Justice William H. Rehnquist (one of Justice Jackson's law clerks) said that "an ability to write clearly has become the most important prerequisite for an American appellate lawyer."[80] The Chief Justice added that "rarely is good oral advocacy sufficient to overcome the impression made by a poorly written brief."[81]

"[T]he purpose of all legal writing," explained U.S. Circuit Judge Ruggero J. Aldisert, "is persuasion. Without clear writing, communication is lessened. To the extent that we diminish communication, we dilute our powers of persuasion."[82]

THE FOUR FUNDAMENTALS IN PERSPECTIVE

Historian Richard Brookhiser calls Abraham Lincoln "one of the greatest writers in the American canon—certainly the greatest ever to reach the White House (Jefferson at his best could be equally good, but his range was narrower)."[83]

Biographer Harold Holzer describes how the President recast Americans' perceptions about effective writing: "Before Lincoln, our leaders spoke in formal, complex sentences cluttered with long words and obscure references to ancient times. Lincoln simplified political writing. He eliminated unnecessary words. He replaced emotion with logic. He made complicated issues clear. He wrote in words everyone could understand— simple words that carried immense power and emotion."[84]

---

[1]   Archibald MacLeish, *Book Note*, 78 Harv. L. Rev. 490, 491 (1964) (reviewing David Mellinkoff, The Language of the Law (1963)).

[2]   Felix Frankfurter, *When Judge Cardozo Writes*, The New Republic, Apr. 8, 1931.

[3]   Oliver Wendell Holmes, *The Profession of the Law*, in Collected Legal Papers 29, 29 (1920).

[4]   Barbara W. Tuchman, Practicing History: Selected Essays 17 (1981).

[5]   Walter Allen, Writers on Writing 210 (2007) (quoting Wells).

[6]   William Shakespeare, The Tragedy of Hamlet, act II, sc. 2.

[7]   Robert Browning, *Andrea del Sarto*, in The Complete Poetic and Dramatic Works of Robert Browning 346, 346 (1895).

[8]   Tim Dick, *Take a Clear Mind and a Sharp Pencil Into Battle Against Verbiage*, Sydney Morning Herald (Australia), Dec. 12, 2009, at 7 (quoting Southey).

[9]   Arthur Penryhn Stanley, D.D., The Life and Correspondence of Thomas Arnold, D.D. 331 (1877) (quoting Arnold).

[10]   Henry Wadsworth Longfellow, *Elegiac Verse*, stanza XIV, http://www.hwlongfellow.org/poems_poem.php?pid=310 (visited Aug. 15, 2020).

[11]   Western Mail (Cardiff, Wales), May 20, 2008, at 17 (quoting Sarnoff).

[12]   James Stavridis, Sailing True North: Ten Admirals and the Voyage of Character xii (2019).

[13]   The Wicked Wit of Winston Churchill 19 (Dominique Enright ed., 2001).

[14]   Bill Moyers, Fooling With Words: A Celebration of Poets and Their Craft xiv (1999).

[15]   Alexander Pope, An Essay on Criticism, lines 109–10.

[16]   John W. Davis, *The Argument of an Appeal*, 26 A.B.A. J. 895, 895 (1940).

[17]   George Rossman, *Appellate Practice and Advocacy*, 16 F.R.D. 403, 407 (1955) (quoting Davis).

[18]   John W. Davis, *supra* note 16 at 897.

[19]   Bryan A. Garner, *Interviews with United States Supreme Court Justices: Chief Justice John G. Roberts, Jr.*, 13 Scribes J. Legal Writing 35 (2010); *see also, e.g.*, Bryan A. Garner, *Interviews with United States Supreme Court Justices: Justice Stephen G. Breyer, id.* at 167 (2010) (most briefs are "[t]oo long. Don't try to put in everything").

[20]   Benjamin Cardozo, The Nature of the Judicial Process 127 (1921).

[21]   Robert H. Jackson, *Advocacy Before the Supreme Court: Suggestions for Effective Case Presentations* 37 A.B.A. J. 801, 803 (1951).

[22]   Patricia M. Wald, *19 Tips From 19 Years On the Appellate Bench*, 1 J. App. Prac. & Process 7, 9 (1999).

[23]   *Id.* at 10.

[24]   Richard Nordquist, *'We Can Do Better': Dr. Seuss on Writing, About Education*, http://grammarandrhetoric.com/blog/index.php/2017/08/27/dr-seuss-on-writing-we-can-do-better   (Aug. 27, 2017) (visited Aug. 10, 2020).

[25]   Blaise Pascal, *Lettres Provinciales*, in Oxford Treasury of Sayings and Quotations 256 (4th ed. 2011).

[26]   The Wicked Wit of Winston Churchill, *supra* note 13 at 45.

[27]   James Stavridis, *supra* note 12 at 112.

[28]   Justice Elena Kagan, *Interview With Bryan A. Garner*, www.lawprose.org (video, part 4) (July 15, 2015).

[29]   Oliva v. Nat'l City Corp., No. 2:08-cv-01559, 2011 WL 32481, at *1 n.1 (D. Nev. Jan. 5, 2011).

[30]   Henry Wadsworth Longfellow, *supra* note 10.

[31]   Cindy Skrzycki, *Government Experts Tackle Bad Writing*, Wash. Post, June 26, 1998, at F1 ("most valuable," quoting Jefferson) (internal quotations omitted); The Family Letters of Thomas Jefferson 369 (E.M. Betts and J.A. Bear, Jr. eds., 1966) (letter of Dec. 7, 1818) ("stile of writing").

[32]   William Strunk Jr. & E.B. White, The Elements of Style 23 (4th ed. 2000).

[33]   I Lloyd Albert Johnson, A Toolbox for Humanity: More Than 9000 Years of Thought 33 (2003) (quoting Cicero).

[34]   Tony Spencer-Smith, The Essentials of Great Writing xx (2015) (quoting Johnson).

[35]   David Mellinkoff, Legal Writing: Sense and Nonsense 128 (1982).

[36]   John S. Friedman, *The Art of Fiction LXXIX: Elie Wiesel*, in Elie Wiesel: Conversations 72 (Robert Franciosi ed., 2002).

[37]   *Id.*

[38]   *Interview by Elizabeth Gaffney & Benjamin Ryder Howe with David McCullough* (Fall 1999), http://www.theparisreview.org/interviews/894/the-art-of-biography-no-2-david-mccullough (visited Aug. 10, 2020).

[39]   Michael Burlingame, *Abraham Lincoln: Family Life* (Miller Center of Public Affairs).

[40]   Catherine Drinker Bowen, Yankee From Olympus: Justice Holmes and His Family 324 (1944).

[41]   David Herbert Donald, Lincoln 464 (1995).

[42]   Ralph Waldo Emerson, *Abraham Lincoln, in* The Selected Writings of Ralph Waldo Emerson 919 (Brooks Atkinson ed., 1940).

[43]   Gabor Borritt, The Gettysburg Gospel: The Lincoln Speech That Nobody Knows 159 (2006) (quoting Stowe).

[44]   James M. McPherson, Abraham Lincoln and the Second American Revolution 112 (1991).

[45]   *Abraham Lincoln: Family Life, supra* note 39.

[46]   Joseph Story, *The Science of Government, in* The Miscellaneous Writings of Joseph Story 622 (William W. Story ed., 1852).

[47]   Wiley B. Rutledge, *The Appellate Brief*, 28 A.B.A. J. 251, 254 (1942).

[48]   Barbara W. Tuchman, *supra* note 4 at 38, 39.

[49]   George D. Gopen, Writing From a Legal Perspective 1 (West 1981).

[50]   Jay Wishingrad & Douglas E. Abrams, *Book Review*, 1981 Duke L.J. 1061,1063 (reviewing George D. Gopen, Writing From a Legal Perspective (West 1981)).

[51]   Sandra Day O'Connor, Out of Order: Stories from the History of the Supreme Court xvii (2013) (quoting Stephen M. Shapiro, *Oral Arguments in the Supreme Court: The Felt Necessities of the Time,* in Yearbook of the Supreme Court Historical Soc'y 22 (1985)).

[52]   Sandra Day O'Connor, *supra* note 51 at 87.

[53]   Walter Allen, *supra* note 5 at 93 (quoting Coleridge).

[54]   Guy de Maupassant, Selected Short Stories 10–11 (Roger Colet ed., 1971) (quoting French writer Gustave Flaubert).

[55]   Felix Frankfurter, *Some Reflections On the Reading of Statutes*, 47 Colum. L. Rev. 527, 528 (1947), *reprinting* Felix Frankfurter, *Sixth Annual Benjamin N. Cardozo Lecture*, 2 Rec. Bar Ass'n City of N.Y., No. 6 (1947).

[56]   Edward H. Levi, An Introduction to Legal Reasoning 1, 6 (1949).

[57]   *Reporters' Notebook: Bits and Pieces of News*, Buffalo News, Sept. 15, 2008, at B2 (quoting Taft).

[58]   Mark Twain, Mark My Words, Mark Twain on Writing 6 (Mark Dawidziak ed., 1996).

[59]   Plato, The Republic, Book III, at 401 (Benjamin Jowett 3d ed. 1991).

[60]   *Brave New World*, The Independent (London), Sept. 24, 2000, at 1 (quoting Coleridge).

[61]   Josiah H. Gilbert, Dictionary of Burning Words of Brilliant Writers: A Cyclopaedia of Quotations 544 (1895) (quoting Emerson).

[62]   Herbert Baxter Adams, Thomas Jefferson and the University of Virginia 58 n.1 (1888) (quoting Jefferson's letter of Sept. 9, 1817).

[63]   *See, e.g., Fast Money*, The Age (Melbourne, Australia), Nov. 29, 1999, at 2 (quoting Einstein).

[64]   Albert Einstein, *Herbert Spencer Lecture at Oxford University* (June 10, 1933), *reprinted in* Albert Einstein, *On the Method of Theoretical Physics*, 1 Phil. of Sci. 163, 165 (1934) ("[T]he supreme goal of all theory is to make the irreducible basic elements as simple and as few as possible without having to surrender the adequate representation of a single datum of experience."); Bryan A. Garner, A Dictionary of Modern Legal Usage 630–31 (3d ed. 2009) ("Albert Einstein once said that his goal in stating an idea was to make it as simple as possible but no simpler.").

[65]   Nomi Prins, *Deck Is Stacked Against Small Banks*, Newsday, Oct. 22, 2009, at A37 (quoting Einstein).

[66]   Paul A. Samuelson & William D. Nordhaus, Economics viii, xiii (12th ed. 1985).

[67]   Manuel L. Real, *Symposium on Mass Torts: What Evil Have We Wrought: Class Action, Mass Torts, and Settlement*, 31 Loy. L.A. L. Rev. 437, 437 (1998) (quoting Churchill).

[68]   Stephen King, On Writing: A Memoir of the Craft 117 (2000).

[69]   A.E. Hotchner, Papa Hemingway: A Personal Memoir 69 (1966) (quoting Hemingway).

[70]   *Id.* at 69–70 (quoting Hemingway); *see also, e.g.,* Kurt Vonnegut, Jr., *The Latest Word*, N.Y. Times, Oct. 30, 1966, at BR1 (reviewing The Random House Dictionary of the English

Language (1966)) ("I wonder now what Ernest Hemingway's dictionary looked like, since he got along so well with dinky words that everybody can spell and truly understand.").

71   H.W. Fowler, A Dictionary of Modern English Usage 344 (2d ed. rev. by Sir Ernest Gowers 1985).

72   *Id.* at 342.

73   Albert Jack, It's a Wonderful Word: The Real Origins of Our Favourite Words 1 (2012) (quoting Evans); *see also, e.g.,* Barbara W. Tuchman, *supra* note 4 at 16–17 ("[S]hort words are always preferable to long ones; the fewer syllables the better, and monosyllables, beautiful and pure . . . , are the best of all.").

74   Richard Lederer, *Foreword*, Robert Hartwell Fiske, The Dictionary of Concise Writing: 10,000 Alternatives to Wordy Phrases 9 (2006) (quoting Twain).

75   W. Brad Johnson & Charles R. Ridley, The Elements of Ethics for Professionals 91 (2008) (quoting Yeats); *see also, e.g.,* Mark Twain, *supra* note 60 at 35 ("Plain clarity is better than ornate obscurity.").

76   Dave Kemper et al., Fusion: Integrated Reading and Writing, Book 2 138 (2014).

77   John Dryden, *Preface* to *Fables, Ancient and Modern, in* Prefaces and Prologues 10 (Charles W. Elliot ed., 2001).

78   Peter Harvey, Reminiscences and Anecdotes of Daniel Webster 118 (1921).

79   Douglas v. Jeannette, 319 U.S. 157, 182 (1943) (Jackson J., concurring).

80   William H. Rehnquist, *From Webster to Word-Processing: The Ascendance of the Appellate Brief*, 1 J. App. Prac. & Process 1, 3 (1999).

81   *Id.* at 4.

82   Ruggero J. Aldisert, Opinion Writing 118 (3d ed. 2012).

83   Richard Brookhiser, W*hat Would Lincoln Do?: Modern-Day Leaders Could Learn a Lot From Our 16th President*, Wall St. J. (Feb. 14, 2014).

84   Harold Holzer, Lincoln—The Writer 18 (2000).

CHAPTER 6

BREAKING THE RULES

■ ■ ■

The four fundamentals explored in Chapter 5—conciseness, precision, simplicity, and clarity—qualify as rules of good writing. So do generally accepted conventions of grammar, syntax, and style. Practices such as writing sentence fragments, splitting infinitives, starting sentences with conjunctions, or ending sentences with prepositions sometimes raise purists' eyebrows as apparent rules violations.

Rules of good writing deserve adherence most of the time because they earned their pedigrees from the time-tested expectations of accomplished writers and diverse readers. But British novelist and essayist George Orwell recognized that "the worst thing one can do with words is to surrender to them."[1] For years, I have taught students that legal writers should be the masters of language, and not its prisoners.

Orwell instructed that writers sometimes communicate most effectively when rules of good writing yield to what lawyers might call a Rule of Reason that permits departures. In *The Elements of Style*, Strunk and White express the formula: "[T]he best writers sometimes disregard the rules of rhetoric," but "unless he is certain of doing as well, [the writer] will probably do best to follow the rules."[2]

GEORGE ORWELL'S RULES

Like other Americans, lawyers remember George Orwell most for his signature novels, *Animal Farm* and *1984*. Less known is Orwell's lifelong passion for the craft of writing, fueled by (as journalist Christopher Hitchens described) his "near visceral feeling for the English language."[3] By urging writers to simplify their expression, Orwell provided impetus for the plain English movement, which began in earnest by the early 1970s and still influences lawyers today.

Orwell's most penetrating commentary about writing appeared in his classic 1946 essay, *Politics and the English Language*, which Judge Richard A. Posner calls "[t]he best style 'handbook'" for legal writers.[4] Nobel Prize-winning economist Paul Krugman calls the essay a resource that "anyone who cares at all about either politics or writing should know by heart."[5] Federal and state judges still cite Orwell's essay to chide colleagues or counsel for calculated imprecision or obfuscation.[6]

To help stem what Orwell called "the decay of language,"[7] the essay advances six rules. Chapter 5 has already discussed two, which are grounded in simplicity and conciseness respectively: "Never use a long word where a short one will do," and "If it is possible to cut a word out, always cut it out."[8] Orwell similarly prefaced three of his remaining four rules with the absolutes "never" or "always":

> *"Never use a metaphor, simile, or other figure of speech*
> *which you are used to seeing in print."*[9]

This rule targets clichés that might entertain, divert, and perhaps even convince readers by displacing analysis with casual acceptance.[10] "By using stale metaphors, similes and idioms," said Orwell, "you save much mental effort, at the cost of leaving your meaning vague, not only for your reader but for yourself."[11] He provided a number of examples, including "run roughshod over," "no axe to grind," and "fishing in troubled waters."[12]

U.S. Circuit Judge Stephen R. Reinhardt referenced this rule in *Eminence Capital, LLC v. Aspeon, Inc.*, a securities fraud class action.[13] The Ninth Circuit held that the district court had improperly dismissed, without leave to amend, the first amended consolidated complaint for failure to state a claim. The panel rejected the district court's conclusion that the plaintiffs already had "three bites at the apple."[14]

Noting that the district court did not cite or apply any of the well-established factors that would have supported dismissal without leave to amend, Judge Reinhardt's concurrence warned against "[t]he problem of clichés as a substitute for rational analysis."[15] "The interpretation and application of statutes, rules, and case law frequently depend on whether we can discriminate among subtle differences of meaning. The biting of apples does not help us."[16] "It is long past time," Judge Reinhardt wrote, "that we learned the lesson Orwell sought to teach us."[17]

> *"Never use the passive where you can use the active."*[18]

This rule instructs that the passive voice can generate unnecessary verbiage, leave readers unsure about who did what to whom, and abandon forceful expression for the soft. Novelist Stephen King finds the passive voice usually "weak," "circuitous," and "frequently tortuous."[19]

Two historical markers make the point. As a beginner legal research and writing instructor in 1979, I invited students to consider how Thomas Jefferson invigorated the second sentence of the Declaration of Independence by opening with the active voice: "*We hold these truths to be self-evident*, that all men are created equal, that they are endowed by their Creator with certain unalienable rights, that among these are life, liberty and the pursuit of happiness." Would Jefferson have rallied the colonists and captivated future generations if he began the sentence instead with the passive: "These truths are held by us to be self-evident. . . ."?

Fast-forward to Inauguration Day on March 4, 1933, when President Franklin D. Roosevelt marshalled the despairing nation's vitality and resilience in the depths of the Great Depression. "[T]he only thing we have to fear is fear itself," he told his fellow Americans in a steady voice.

Much of the immortality of President Roosevelt's iconic sentence stems from its delivery at an Inauguration, the quadrennial American ritual whose pomp and circumstance attracts millions around the world. But immortality here stems from more than FDR's commanding presence on the national stage at a moment of profound crisis. In video recordings and on the printed page,[20] FDR's sentence also endures because of its force and content.

The national reaction to the Inaugural Address was immediate. "You could see tears streaming down people's faces" in the crowd as FDR reinvigorated the national spirit, reported one historian.[21] Early in the 1932 campaign, influential columnist Walter Lippmann had dismissed Roosevelt as a "pleasant man . . . without any important qualification for office."[22] But when he heard the President's frontal assault on fear, Lippmann struck a different chord. "The inauguration of Mr. Roosevelt," he wrote, "has brought to the Presidency a man who . . . has instantly captured the confidence of the people."[23]

FDR's faceoff with fear was vigorous and defiant, but it was not entirely new. Cicero, William Shakespeare, Sir Francis Bacon, Daniel Defoe, Lord Chesterfield, and William James had written earlier about fear's emotional toll,[24] but no evidence emerged that the President or any of his aides knew what they had said.

A likely source of FDR's inspirational "fear" sentence was an anthology of Henry David Thoreau's writings, which a friend of Eleanor Roosevelt gave the President-Elect late in February as he applied the finishing touches to his upcoming address.[25] Another possible source sometimes advanced is a statement by the chairman of the U.S. Chamber of Commerce, which appeared prominently in a front-page *New York Times* article in February, 1931 and might have caught the eye of Roosevelt aide Louis Howe as it gained some currency in the business world.[26]

From one source or the other, Roosevelt crafted a more robust, passionate statement that rejuvenated the American spirit. Thoreau and the Chamber of Commerce chairman had spoken in the passive voice, sentences laden with verbiage and indirection. "Nothing is so much to be feared as fear," wrote Thoreau.[27] "In a condition of this kind," said the chairman, "the thing to be feared most is fear itself."[28]

Would FDR have stirred the stricken nation with similar passivity and verbal baggage, broadcast to millions on the radio and published in newspapers and magazines from coast to coast? Decades after the national crisis had passed, would a stodgy Presidential invocation remain a distinct cultural marker in the 21st century?

> *"Never use a foreign phrase, a scientific word, or a jargon word if*
> *you can think of an everyday English equivalent."*[29]

Jargon is the subject of Chapter 11. Discussion of careless use of foreign expressions appears here.

Lincoln biographer David Herbert Donald reported that when the President prepared the Gettysburg Address in 1863, he "chose his words deliberately, preferring, as he always did, short words to long, words of Anglo-Saxon origin to those of Latin derivation."[30] Then as now, legal writers sometimes assumed that foreign words and foreign phrases impress readers. Lincoln assumed the contrary. These foreign sources might inflate the writer's ego with an aura of perceived sophistication, but they can also impose easily avoidable barriers that perplex and annoy readers.

Readers confronted with unfamiliar foreign words will more likely roll their eyes, guess at meaning, or skip over the passage entirely. Some readers may wonder whether the lawyer seeks to show off, or even to shroud a weak argument. Lawyers appear most confident when they fortify lines of communication, not fracture them.

Few readers will scurry to a law dictionary to learn what terms such as *inter alia, a fortiori,* or *ratio decidendi* mean. Why not write "among other things," "with stronger reason," or "the rationale for the court's decision"? Legal rights and obligations frequently turn on complex doctrine, even without the writer's needlessly strewing roadblocks in the reader's path.

Orwell was right that nearly every foreign phrase has a more readily understandable English language counterpart, and that English speaking readers usually respond more readily to the counterpart. Justice Robert H. Jackson, one of the Supreme Court's most talented writers, said that the skillful advocate "will master the short Saxon word that pierces the mind like a spear and the simple figure that lights the understanding. He will never drive the judge to his dictionary."[31]

Poet Robert Bly says that poetry should use "words . . . you could speak to your friends."[32] So should prose. Lawyers would not use *inter alia, a fortiori, ratio decidendi,* or similar linguistic atrocities in a social gathering with professional or lay guests, so lawyers should not use them in formal writing either.

THE RULE OF REASON

Orwell introduced each rule discussed above with "never" or "always." Law students and lawyers learn to approach such commands gingerly because they know that few rules support absolutes. Orwell closed with a final rule, a Rule of Reason:

> *"Break any of these rules sooner than say*
> *anything outright barbarous."*[33]

As lawyers strive for effective writing, Orwell left room for purposeful rules violations that facilitate communication with readers. The writer determines whether sufficient reason exists for breaking a rule, but the "outright barbarous" test sets the bar too high. Three of Orwell's own rules illustrate why, even short of expression "outright barbarous,"[34] skillful writers sometimes apply a Rule of Reason rather than become prisoners of language.

Metaphors, Similes, and Similar Figures of Speech

Orwell instructs that indiscriminate use of metaphors and similar figures of speech (such as "run roughshod over" or "fishing in troubled waters") can lull writers and readers into complacency that displaces rigorous analysis. But careful use of figures of speech can also bolster legal writing with vivid imagery that complements analysis without substituting for it.

"Think of the poor judge who is reading . . . hundreds and hundreds of these briefs," says Chief Justice Roberts.[35] "Liven up their life just a little bit . . . with something interesting."[36] "It helps to break the monotony of the printed legal page to add a bit of life now and then," explained Justice Wiley B. Rutledge.[37]

The Passive Voice

Orwell instructs, "Never use the passive where you can use the active." The passive voice, however, sometimes plays a worthwhile or even essential role in lawyers' writing. For example, a lawyer may have sound reasons for leaving the sentence's subject indefinite, even at the expense of adding a few words to the sentence: "Decisions were discussed that led to the building's collapse." The lawyer might not know who participated in the decision making, might not want to risk defaming anyone by casting blame prematurely, might want to spur further investigation, or might want to protect a client. The wrongdoers' identities might not be essential, at least for now.

Recall too the second sentence from the Declaration of Independence, quoted above. Jefferson deftly used the passive voice ("that they are endowed by their Creator with certain unalienable rights. . . ."). The active voice ("that their Creator endowed them with") would not have produced expression "outright barbarous," but it would have sacrificed rhythm and cadence that strengthened Jefferson's message. I explain to my legal history students that the passive voice left no doubt about who did the endowing, and that a few extra words did not slow readers or otherwise cloud the Declaration's message.

Foreign Phrases and the Like

Orwell's instructs, "Never use a foreign phrase . . . if you can think of an everyday English equivalent." But the Rule of Reason says that where a foreign phrase qualifies as a legal term of art, the lawyer may advance conciseness, precision, simplicity, and clarity by using it to reach an audience of lawyers who presumably understand the meaning.

If a legal writer wants to explain the binding or persuasive force of a judicial precedent, for example, an audience of lawyers will readily understand what *stare decisis* means, even without explanation or translation from Latin. Among lawyers, the phrase has become a term of art.

But the phrase may escape most lay readers, so saying "a system of precedent," together with any further explanation the writer deems useful, would seem wiser. The alternative is likely wordier, but conciseness sometimes yields to the Rule of Reason. When in doubt, legal writers should hedge their bets: "Some law requires technical words," said leading plain English advocate David Mellinkoff, but "[h]ardly any law forbids explaining them."[38]

"ARRANT PEDANTRY"

Grounded in instinct and common sense, the Rule of Reason holds a prominent place in good writing. Robert MacNeil, longtime co-anchor of the MacNeil/Lehrer NewsHour on the Public Broadcasting System (PBS), explains why: "The English-speaking peoples have defeated all efforts to build fences around their language, to defer to an academy on what was permissible English and what not. They'll decide for themselves, thanks just the same. Nothing better expresses resistance to arbitrary authority than the persistence of what grammarians have denounced for centuries as 'errors.' "[39]

Legal writers may find ample reason to enhance meaning or style by, for example, writing a sentence fragment, splitting an infinitive, starting a sentence with a conjunction, or ending a sentence with a preposition. Enhancing communication remains preferable to following "arbitrary authority" from stylebooks that readers do not examine. More than two generations of Star Trek fans have not tarried over the split infinitive that opened the legendary show: "To boldly go where no man has gone before."

Sir Winston Churchill was a statesman who also received the Nobel Prize in Literature as a prolific, graceful writer. When a critic chastised the versatile wartime leader for sometimes ending sentences with prepositions, he reportedly had a tart reply: "That is the sort of arrant pedantry up with which I shall not put."[40]

---

1   George Orwell, *Politics and the English Language*, in Essays on Language and Usage 325, 335 (Leonard F. Dean & Kenneth G. Wilson eds., 2d ed. 1963), available at http://orwell.ru/library/essays/politics/english/e_polit (visited Aug. 11, 2020). *See also, e.g.*, Benjamin Dreyer, Dreyer's English: An Utterly Correct Guide to Clarity and Style 7 (2019) (" 'rules of the English Language] are meant to be broken'—once you've learned them. . . .").

2   William Strunk Jr. & E.B. White, The Elements of Style xvii–xviii (4th ed. 2000); *see also* William Strunk Jr., The Elements of Style 2 (2014).

3   Christopher Hitchens, *The Importance of Being Orwell*, Vanity Fair (July 31, 2012).

4   Richard A. Posner, *Judges' Writing Styles (And Do They Matter?)*, 62 U. Chi. L. Rev. 1421, 1423 n.8 (1995); *see also* Richard A. Posner, Divergent Paths 338 (2016) (calling Orwell's essay "indispensable").

5   Paul Krugman, *Orwell, China, and Me*, N.Y. Times Blogs (July 20, 2013), http://krugman.blogs.nytimes.com/2013/07/20/orwell-china-and-me/ (visited Aug. 10, 2020).

6   *E.g.*, National Ass'n of Regulatory Utility Comm'rs v. U.S. Dep't of Energy, 680 F.3d 819, 820 n.1 (D.C. Cir. 2012), discussed in Chapter 12; Grutter v. Bollinger, 288 F.3d 732, 774 (6th Cir. 2002) (en banc) (Boggs, J., dissenting), *aff'd*, 539 U.S. 306 (2003); Anthony A. Gagliano & Co. v. Openfirst, LLC, 828 N.W.2d 268, 271 n.2 (Wis. Ct. App. 2013); Palm Beach Cnty. Sheriff v. State, 854 So.2d 278, 282 (Fla. Dist. Ct. App. 2003).

7   George Orwell, *supra* note 1, at 336.

8   *Id*. at 335.

9   *Id*.

10   H.W. Fowler, A Dictionary of Modern English Usage 90–91 (2d ed. rev. by Sir Ernest Gowers 1985) (defining "cliché").

11   George Orwell, *supra* note 1, at 331–32.

12   *Id*. at 327.

13   316 F.3d 1048, 1053 (9th Cir. 2003) (Reinhardt, J., concurring).

14   *Id*.

15   *Id*. at 1054.

16   *Id*.

17   *Id*.

18   George Orwell, *supra* note 1, at 335.

19   Stephen King, On Writing: A Memoir of the Craft 123 (2000).

20   *Franklin Delano Roosevelt: First Inaugural Address* (text and video), http://www.americanrhetoric.com/speeches/fdrfirstinaugural.html (visited May 1, 2020).

21   Ted Morgan, Roosevelt: A Biography 375 (1985), also reported in Max Hastings, *Franklin D Roosevelt: The Man Who Conquered Fear*, The Independent (London, U.K.), Jan. 19, 2009.

22   Max Hastings, *supra* note 21.

23   Arthur A. Ekirch, Jr., Ideologies and Utopias: The Impact of the New Deal on American Thought 91 (1969) (quoting Lippmann).

24   Jonathan Alter, The Defining Moment: FDR's Hundred Days and the Triumph of Hope 211 (2006).

25   *Id*. at 210–11; Kenneth C. Davis, Don't Know Much About History 350 (2d ed. 2003); Nathan Miller, FDR: An Intimate History 303 (1983).

26   Jonathan Alter, *supra* note 24 at 211.

27   *Id*.

28   *Id*.; Adam Cohen, Nothing to Fear: FDR's Inner Circle and the Hundred Days that Created Modern America 39 (2009).

29   George Orwell, *supra* note 1 at 335.

30   David Herbert Donald, Lincoln 461 (1995).

31   Robert Jackson, *Advocacy Before the Supreme Court: Suggestions for Effective Case Preparation*, 37 A.B.A. J. 801, 863–64 (1951).

---

32 Quoted in Bill Moyers, The Language of Life: A Festival of Poets 60 (1995).

33 George Orwell, *supra* note 1 at 335.

34 H.W. Fowler, *supra* note 10 at 48–49 (defining barbarism, barbarity, barbarousness, and barbarisms).

35 Bryan A. Garner, *Interviews with Supreme Court Justices: Chief Justice John G. Roberts, Jr.,* 13 Scribes J. Legal Writing 51, 57 (2010) (quoting Chief Justice Roberts).

36 *Id.*

37 Wiley B. Rutledge, *The Appellate Brief*, 28 A.B.A. J. 251, 254–55 (1942).

38 David Mellinkoff, Legal Writing: Sense and Nonsense 65 (1982).

39 Robert MacNeil, Wordstruck 220 (1989).

40 Susan E. Rowe, *Six to Nix: Grammar Rules to Leave Behind*, 67 Or. St. Bar Bull. 37 (Nov. 2006) (quoting Churchill).

CHAPTER 7

REASON AND PASSION IN PERSUASIVE LEGAL WRITING

■ ■ ■

Good writing marked by the civility urged in Chapter 2 does not mean toothless writing that might compromise the lawyer's client or cause.[1] The adversary system of civil and criminal justice depends on lawyers who deliver persuasive writing accented not only by civility, but also by reason and passion.

Reason and passion shaped ancient rhetoric, influenced the writings of our nation's Founders, and remain prominent in contemporary American law and culture. In persuasive legal writing, "reason" loosely means careful application of relevant doctrine to the facts. "Passion" loosely means vigorous argument that advances the position.

Reason and passion marked this chapter's example, Justice Robert H. Jackson's majority opinion in *West Virginia State Board of Education v. Barnette* (1943), the Supreme Court's second flag salute case.[2] In the midst of World War II, *Barnette* held that Jehovah's Witnesses schoolchildren and their families enjoyed a First Amendment speech right to refuse to salute the flag or recite the Pledge of Allegiance, acts that they said would violate their religious beliefs.

A majority opinion laden with arid formalism would have decided *Barnette*, but also would have blunted the decision's immediate influence and left its drama largely forgotten decades later. Instead, Justice Jackson wrote what Judge Richard A. Posner says "may be the most eloquent majority opinion in the history of the Supreme Court."[3]

This chapter briefly surveys the impact of reason and passion on expression from ancient times, and then displays Justice Jackson's harnessing of these two complementary forces in *Barnette*. The chapter concludes by discussing how the two forces can energize lawyers' written advocacy today.

BARNETTE

Barnette's story began in early January of 1942, barely a month after Japan attacked the U.S. Pacific naval fleet at Pearl Harbor. Historian David McCullough recalls these days as "[a]mong the darkest times in recent memory."[4] "Hitler's armies were nearly to Moscow; ... German submarines were sinking our oil tankers off the coasts of Florida and New Jersey, within sight of the beaches, and there was not a thing we could do about it; ... half our navy had been destroyed at Pearl Harbor. We had scarcely any air force. Army recruits were drilling with wooden rifles. And there was no guarantee whatever that the Nazi war machine could be stopped."[5]

In the weeks following Pearl Harbor, patriotic appeals to young and old spread swiftly. On January 9, 1942, the West Virginia State Board of Education followed several other state and local school authorities by requiring public school students and teachers to salute the flag and recite the Pledge of Allegiance daily. By permitting no exemptions for religious objection, the requirement's brunt fell heavily on Jehovah's Witnesses schoolchildren, whose families refused to comply on the ground that salute and recitation were acts of idolatry that violated Biblical commands.

Noncompliant West Virginia children faced expulsion from school, plus delinquency proceedings that threatened confinement in juvenile reformatories. One study condemned these austere juvenile institutions as "incompatible with human dignity, . . . a black record of human tragedy, of social and economic waste, of gross brutality, crass stupidity, totalitarian regimentation . . . and a corroding monotony even deadlier than physical violence."[6] Parents risked imprisonment for violating compulsory education acts, plus sanctions for child neglect that might result in temporary or permanent loss of custody.[7]

In West Virginia and elsewhere, public school authorities stood on solid constitutional ground because in *Minersville School District v. Gobitis* in 1940, the Supreme Court had upheld mandatory flag salutes and Pledge recitation against Witness' claims of religious objection.[8] As many as 2000 Witnesses children were expelled from school, and many parents landed in criminal court.[9]

Gobitis also unleashed a national wave of vigilantism against the Witnesses, who appeared disloyal or even treasonous to Americans who perceived the salute and Pledge recitation as solemn obligations with war clouds looming. Witnesses' families suffered beatings, physical intimidation, and property destruction from angry mobs, often while local sheriffs and other law enforcement officers watched with approval, not intervening to secure the victims' safety.[10]

With unmistakable symbolism, and with ultimate victory over the Axis powers still uncertain, *Barnette* overruled *Gobitis* on Flag Day, June 14, 1943. Justice Jackson's majority opinion deftly combined reason and passion, dual forces with an imposing pedigree for energizing written expression.

BALANCING REASON AND PASSION

The pedigree began as early as Plato's *Republic*, which asked whether "passion [is] different from reason," and concluded that "the one ruling principle of reason [is] that reason ought to rule."[11] "The law," wrote Aristotle, "is reason[ ] free from passion."[12]

In colonial North America, impulses to balance reason and passion guided George Washington's personal and public life. As a schoolboy not yet 16, he had fulfilled a school exercise by copying 110 "Rules of Civility and Decent Behaviour in Company and Conversation," drawn from an English translation of a book compiled by French Jesuits in the late 1500s.[13] The 58th Rule of Civility left a lasting impression on the future President's upbringing and public outlook: "[I]n all Causes of Passion admit Reason to Govern."[14]

In 1783, General Washington learned that some of his officers planned to press grievances against Congress, which had not paid them promised salaries or pensions. His Newburgh Address dissuaded the officers from pursuing the plan, which he condemned as "addressed more to the feelings of passions than to the reason & judgment of the army."[15] In his Farewell Address in 1796, Washington warned the nation not to "adopt[ ] through passion what reason would reject."[16]

The balance between reason and passion helped shape early American political writing, most prominently several of the *Federalist* essays written by Alexander Hamilton, James Madison, and John Jay in 1787 and 1788 to advocate ratification of the Constitution. *Federalist No. 49*, for example, argued for avoiding frequent future constitutional conventions, where "the *passions . . .* not *the reason*, of the public, would sit in judgment."[17]

As one of history's great political philosophers and as an opponent of the Federalists, Thomas Jefferson likely knew the writings of the ancient Greeks and surely knew the influence of the *Federalist* essays. "Let nothing be spared of either reason or passion," he wrote in 1809, "to preserve the public confidence entire, as the only rock of our safety."[18]

In one of his earliest published speeches, delivered in 1838, 29-year-old lawyer Abraham Lincoln criticized a rash of lynchings for reflecting a "growing disposition to substitute the wild and furious passions in lieu of the sober judgment of the courts."[19] "Passion has helped us" by igniting the Revolution that won independence from Britain, Lincoln explained, but unrestrained passion "will in future be our enemy. Reason, cold, calculating, unimpassioned reason, must furnish all the materials for our future support and defence."[20]

Abolitionist leader and former slave Frederick Douglass wrote more generally about racial justice in 1855: "There is no relation more unfavorable to the development of honorable character, than that sustained by the slaveholder to the slave. Reason is imprisoned here, and passions run wild."[21]

In more recent times, voices in public policy debates and cultural discussion frequently urge accommodation between reason and passion.[22] During the House Judiciary Committee's Watergate hearings that led to President Nixon's resignation in 1974, for example, Representative Barbara Jordan of Texas riveted the nation with her opening statement that "reason, and not passion . . . must guide our deliberations, guide our debate, and guide our decision."[23] Speaking to the La Jolla (Calif.) Music Society three decades later, Justice Sandra Day O'Connor said that law and music each represent "a fusion of reason and passion."[24]

Discussing his own religious upbringing in his first memoir, *Dreams from My Father* (1995), lawyer and Senator Barack Obama wrote that his grandmother's family preferred "a straight-backed form of Methodism that valued reason over passion and temperance over both."[25] In *The Audacity of Hope: Thoughts on Reclaiming the American Dream* (2006), the future President wrote that "the Constitution envisions a road map by which we marry passion to reason, the ideal of individual freedom to the demands of community."[26]

In 2017, Senator John McCain acknowledged that "[s]ometimes I've let my passion rule my reason. . . . Sometimes I made it harder to find common ground because of something harsh I said to a colleague."[27]

"THE UNANIMITY OF THE GRAVEYARD"

Justice Jackson's majority opinion in *Barnette* demonstrates that balanced reason and passion can invigorate persuasive legal writing. The opinion opened with "reason"—recitation of the facts and relevant First Amendment speech doctrine. Then Justice Jackson turned to "passion," the heart of the opinion whose eloquence has captivated lawyers ever since.

"To enforce [the Bill of Rights] today is not to choose weak government over strong government," Justice Jackson wrote for the six-justice majority that affirmed the unpopular religious group's constitutional rights. "It is only to adhere as a means of strength to individual freedom of mind in preference to officially disciplined uniformity for which history indicates a disappointing and disastrous end."[28]

"The very purpose of a Bill of Rights," Justice Jackson explained, "was to withdraw certain subjects from the vicissitudes of political controversy, to place them beyond the reach of majorities and officials and to establish them as legal principles to be applied by the courts. One's right to life, liberty, and property, to free speech, a free press, freedom of worship and assembly, and other fundamental rights may not be submitted to vote; they depend on the outcome of no elections."[29]

"Those who begin coercive elimination of dissent," Justice Jackson warned, "soon find themselves exterminating dissenters. Compulsory unification of opinion achieves only the unanimity of the graveyard."[30] Calibrated reason and passion determined the rights of the Jehovah's Witnesses schoolchildren:

> To believe that patriotism will not flourish if patriotic ceremonies are voluntary and spontaneous instead of a compulsory routine is to make an unflattering estimate of the appeal of our institutions to free minds. We can have intellectual individualism and the rich cultural diversities that we owe to exceptional minds only at the price of occasional eccentricity and abnormal attitudes. When they are so harmless to others or to the State as those we deal with here, the price is not too great. But freedom to differ is not limited to things that do not matter much. That would be a mere shadow of freedom. The test of its substance is the right to differ as to things that touch the heart of the existing order.[31]

Justice Jackson closed with a passionate endorsement of individual freedom that one commentator calls "the most illuminating definition of Americanism in the history of the Court":[32] "If there is any fixed star in our constitutional constellation, it is that no official, high or petty, can prescribe what shall be orthodox in politics, nationalism, religion, or other matters of opinion or force citizens to confess by word or act their faith therein."[33]

REASON AND PASSION IN LAWYERS' ADVOCACY

Judges hold no monopoly on persuasive balancing of written reason and passion. Nor can the balance invigorate only momentous cases such as *Barnette* and others that land in the Supreme Court. At all levels of the federal and state judiciary, decision making relies on advocates who vigorously raise, frame, and argue issues of fact and law in cases whose importance to the parties may dwarf the outcome's effect on the legal fabric.

Speaking about brief writing, U.S. Circuit Judge Jacques L. Wiener, Jr. instructs that "[j]udges are human . . . so you must demonstrate both why your client should win (the emotional element) and the proper legal way that your client can win (the intellectual element)."[34] "Your written argument should not be devoid of passion, but it must be grounded in logic, legally supported. . . ."[35]

At the Northwestern University School of Law, Chief Justice Roberts told students that legally unsupported boilerplate falls flat. "We get hundreds and hundreds of briefs, and they're all the same," said the Chief Justice. "Somebody says, 'My client clearly deserves to win, the cases clearly do this, the language clearly reads this.' . . . And you pick up the other side and, lo and behold, they think they clearly deserve to win."[36] The

Justices, he suggested, find unpersuasive recitations that rely on a conclusory label such as "clearly" because "if it was an easy case, we wouldn't have it."[37]

The Chief Justice's message is that judges are unlikely to be persuaded by a brief writer's passion, unaccompanied by reason grounded in fact and law, that the client must "clearly" (or "manifestly," "surely," or "certainly") prevail. These unadorned conclusory labels are weak surrogates for reasoned, passionate analysis about why the facts and the law support the client's position.

---

[1]   This chapter is adapted from Douglas E. Abrams, *Justice Jackson and the Second Flag-Salute Case: Reason and Passion in Opinion-Writing,* 36 J. Sup. Ct. Hist. 30 (2011).

[2]   319 U.S. 624 (1943).

[3]   Richard A. Posner, The Problems of Jurisprudence 147 (1990).

[4]   David McCullough, *The Course of Human Events* 1 (2003 Jefferson Lecture In the Humanities), https://www.neh.gov/about/awards/jefferson-lecture-david-mccullough-biography (visited Aug. 10, 2020).

[5]   *Id.*

[6]   Albert Deutsch, Our Rejected Children xix, 162 (1950).

[7]   West Virginia State Board of Education v. Barnette, 319 U.S. at 626, 629–30; *see* Shawn Francis Peters, Judging Jehovah's Witnesses: Religious Persecution and the Dawn of the Rights Revolution 164–77 (2000).

[8]   310 U.S. 586 (1940), *overruled,* West Virginia State Board of Education v. Barnette, 319 U.S. 624 (1943).

[9]   Vincent Blasi & Seana V. Shiffrin, *The Story of West Virginia State Board of Education v. Barnette: The Pledge of Allegiance and the Freedom of Thought,* in Constitutional Law Stories 445 (Michael C. Dorf ed., 2004).

[10]   Shawn Francis Peters, *supra* note 7 at 72–154.

[11]   Plato, The Republic, Book IV, at 159–62 (Benjamin Jowett ed., 1991).

[12]   Aristotle, The Politics of Aristotle 146 (Ernest Baker trans., 1946).

[13]   J.M. Toner, M.D., George Washington's Rules of Civility and Decent Behaviour In Company and Conversation 8 (1888).

[14]   *Id.* at 24.

[15]   David Ramsay, *The Life of George Washington,* Chap. 9 (1807).

[16]   *Washington's Farewell Address (1796),* The Avalon Project, https://avalon.law.yale.edu/18th_century/washing.asp (visited Aug. 10, 2020).

[17]   The Federalist Papers and the New Institutionalism 54 (Bernard Grofman & Donald Wittman eds., 1989) (emphasis in original).

[18]   *Thomas Jefferson to Caesar A. Rodney, 10 Feb. 1810,* Nat'l Archives, https://founders.archives.gov/?q=caesar%20rodney%201810%20jefferson&s=1511311111&sa=&r=10&sr= (visited Aug. 10, 2020).

[19]   Abraham Lincoln, *The Perpetuation of Our Political Institutions: Address Before the Young Men's Lyceum of Springfield, Ill., Jan. 27, 1838,* in Abraham Lincoln: A Documentary Portrait Through His Speeches and Writings 35–36 (Don E. Fehrenbacher ed., 1977).

[20]   *Id.* at 43.

[21]   Frederick Douglass, My Bondage and My Freedom 32 (John Stauffer ed., 2003).

[22]   *See, e.g., When Passion, Not Reason, Rules,* S.F. Chronicle, Aug. 6, 2004, at B8 (editorial) (California's "three strikes" sentencing law).

[23]   Barbara Jordan, *Statement on the Articles of Impeachment,* American Rhetoric, http://www.americanrhetoric.com/speeches/barbarajordanjudiciarystatement.htm (visited Aug. 10, 2020).

[24]   Mark Swed, *Justice O'Connor Fails to Make Case,* L.A. Times, Aug. 14, 2004, at 1.

25   Barack Obama, Dreams from My Father: A Story of Race and Inheritance 14 (2004).

26   Barack Obama, The Audacity of Hope: Thoughts on Reclaiming the American Dream 113 (2008).

27   Lauren Gambino & David Smith, *"John McCain Is Not Fighting a Losing Battle,"* The Guardian (UK), May 12, 2018.

28   Barnette, 319 U.S. at 637.

29   *Id.* at 638.

30   *Id.* at 641.

31   *Id.* at 641–42.

32   Nat Hentoff, Living the Bill of Rights: How To Be an Authentic American 143 (1998).

33   *Barnette*, 319 U.S. at 642.

34   Jacques L. Wiener, Jr., *Ruminations from the Bench: Brief Writing and Oral Argument in the Fifth Circuit*, 70 Tul. L. Rev. 187, 194 (1995).

35   *Id.*

36   Robert Barnes, *Chief Justice Counsels Humility*, Wash. Post, at A15 (Feb. 6, 2007).

37   *Id.*

PART 4

EDITING

■ ■ ■

Biochemist George Wald said that when professionals write, "We are the products of editing, rather than of authorship."[1] Editors may not share the by-line, but their contributions help shape effective legal writing. In the Legal Writer's Theater that Chapter 2 portrays, skilled editors are the supporting cast.

An editor may perform either or both of two roles in the legal writing process. Beginning in the writing's early stages and continuing through later drafts, an editor trained in the law may offer substantive suggestions about doctrine, analysis, or proposed conclusions. Or an editor may proofread for such flaws as inaccurate quotes, incorrect citations, typographical errors, misspellings, and grammatical stresses.

Substantive editors may contribute proofreading, and proofreaders may contribute substantive suggestions. Despite their frequent operation in tandem, the two editorial roles are roughly separated here for the sake of presentation. After describing generally how editorial input can improve lawyers' writing, Chapter 8 emphasizes substantive editing and discusses proofreading only in passing. Chapter 9 continues the emphasis on substance before Chapter 10 turns more directly to proofreading.

---

[1]   George Wald, *The Origin of Optical Activity*, 69 Annals of the N.Y. Acad. of Sci. 352, 367 (1957).

CHAPTER 8

"PERFECT FIRST DRAFTS DON'T EXIST"

■ ■ ■

Before a third-person editor ever weighs in, editing begins with the writer. "There is no such thing as good writing. There is only good re-writing," said Justice Louis D. Brandeis, who sometimes rewrote his draft opinions for substance or style a dozen or more times before the pages satisfied him.[1] A biographer similarly recounts how Abraham Lincoln would "shut himself away to write and rewrite his most important speeches," whose words and sentiments still resound today.[2] Justice Brandeis and President Lincoln demonstrate the writer's own responsibility for what emerges.

"I've never read or written a perfect first draft. Perfect first drafts don't exist," says British novelist and former lawyer M.J. Hyland.[3] "Good writers," she explains, are "humble and self-aware enough to know that revision is always necessary."[4] Biographer Edmund Morris recalls once spending seven hours fashioning one sentence.[5] Similar patience is usually beyond the reach of lawyers who write facing often-stringent time deadlines and financial pressures, but Morris' recollection demonstrates the central role of meticulous self-editing beyond the first draft.

Ernest Hemingway believed that "easy writing makes hard reading,"[6] and he acknowledged that he rewrote the last page of *A Farewell to Arms* 39 times before the ending satisfied him.[7] "I'm not a very good writer, but I'm an excellent rewriter," reported James A. Michener,[8] who could not "recall anything of mine that's ever been printed in less than three drafts."[9]

Good writing often begins with early over-writing, followed by "trimming the fat" during the editorial process. As deadlines approach, writers usually find it easier to cut existing material than to add new material. Dr. Seuss, who wrote for a particularly demanding audience, estimated that "[f]or a 60-page book, I'll probably write 500 pages. . . . I winnow out."[10] "The wastepaper basket is a writer's best friend," said Isaac Bashevis Singer, a Nobel Prize laureate in Literature.[11]

EDITING BY THIRD PERSONS

At some point during the researching and writing process, even a talented writer may be unable alone to apply the finishing touches. The writer may simply miss substantive or proofreading points, or the writer's mind may grow tired as the eyes begin to "see" what the writer thinks is on the page rather than what is actually there.

A third-person editor brings a fresh pair of eyes that can contribute objectivity and perspective. The third person may pinpoint missing links in the substantive chain of logic that escaped the writer, who may have become so intimate with the project that he or she neglected to express each link in writing. The editor may flag arguments that need to be added, deleted, amplified, or tightened.

Editors may also correct spelling and typographical errors, omitted or superfluous words, or tangled phrasing. Words, sentences, and paragraphs may need to be recast more concisely, precisely, simply, and clearly. Syntax, tone, or style may need refinement. Even if the writer has begun to shorten the draft by trimming the fat, further pruning may be necessary to meet maximum page limits specified by court rules, or may be desirable to accommodate the audience's attention span or to strengthen the force of what remains.

EDITING GUIDELINES FOR LAWYERS

The remainder of this chapter presents five guidelines for third-person editing, a process that former *New Yorker* editor Harold W. Ross likened to "quarreling with writers."[12] Quarrels may sometimes characterize relations between writers and editors in the magazine world, but effective legal writing stems from professional cooperation between writer and editor.

1. *Encourage candor.* We law professors thrive on colleagues who edit our drafts, and we relish editing our colleagues' drafts. But when I draft a report or other document as a board member or committee member in the community, I sometimes have to plead for candid editing from members who would otherwise assume that their mark-ups would hurt my feelings.

I want editing, and I assure everyone else on the board or committee that I mean it. I explain that particularly where a prospective editor retains the option to decline service, the editor pays the writer a compliment by devoting valuable time to polishing the draft. No one has ever edited my writing and made it worse. Improvement is the nearly inevitable result.

Lawyers need to deliver this assurance whenever they sense that a prospective editor might otherwise feel reluctant to challenge or to point out shortcomings. Particularly where the editor does not know the lawyer well, or holds a subordinate position in a firm or agency, nods of approval may appear the safest path. Because a lawyer usually engages only one editor or a small number on a project, failure to overcome an editor's initial reticence squanders a valuable resource.

In a sincere tone, the lawyer should encourage candor by asking the editor whether he or she followed the analysis and felt comfortable with its content. Editing, of course, may confirm the soundness of much of what already appears on the page, but sincerity also means expressing gratitude for robust criticism.

Editorial criticism can avoid pitfalls before readers get their hands on the brief or other final document. The editor brings a fresh perspective to the page, but so will the lawyer's readers. Recall from Chapter 5 that "hostile" readers may try their best to find weaknesses in the prose, even perhaps to find ways of turning the words against the lawyer's intended meaning.[13] The editor's early red flags seem preferable to fending off surprises after the lawyer crosses the point of no return with publication.

2. *Decide the best time to seek third-person editing, but do not wait too long.* Normally the writer is in the best position to determine when to begin soliciting editorial input. Timing may depend on such factors as the writer's grasp of the subject matter at various stages, the writer's perceived need for advice, an editor's availability, and the writer's deadline.

With little but an outline, a writer may benefit from early discussion of ideas with one or more editors who help the writer focus. Similar discussion may help when the editor comments on an early draft, while the writer can still sharpen initial points or stake out new directions. Or the writer may wait until the project approaches finality, when an editor can help burnish substance, style, or both.

3. *Seek editors who resemble or understand the intended audience.* Chapter 2 likened legal writers to theater actors because lawyers appear on a virtual stage when we write for an audience. Editing resembles a dress rehearsal, when the lawyer can still refashion the performance before the curtain opens to readers.

Among the most effective editors are people who are likely to react as the lawyer would expect the anticipated audience to react, or people who otherwise understand the audience. An editor with this resemblance or understanding may bring perspectives different than the writer's, but these differences can enhance the final product.

Where a lawyer writes a brief or other court submission, for example, partners or associates make excellent editors. Especially helpful are the law office's former judges and former judicial law clerks, whose experience with confidential decision making equips them with an insider's perspective to fashion sound arguments. The writer's spouse or friend can pitch in if confidentiality guarantees are met. The lawyer may feel comfortable also soliciting review and input from the client, who is a member of the audience, whether or not trained in the law.

4. *Focus on civility*. Chapter 2 explained why effective legal writing means civil writing. Incivility can disserve both client and lawyer, but emotion needing restraint may consciously or subconsciously emerge as the lawyer learns the client's position or seeks to satisfy the client's feelings. Where legal writers sense that they might have approached or crossed the line separating reason and passion from incivility, they may be right. Solicit the editor's candor because words in print often cannot easily be retracted or explained away.

5. *Unless otherwise agreed, do not rely on editors to do the writing*. Presumably the lawyer knows the subject better than the editor does because the writer has lived with it longer. If an editor suggests adding or deleting a passage, the lawyer might invite the editor to draft a short rewrite. But in the absence of a contrary agreement or understanding that ethically enlists an editor to assume an author's role, lawyers should resist temptation to conscript the editor as an unacknowledged ghost writer.

Successful lawyers tend to maintain busy schedules but, to paraphrase President Harry S. Truman, the buck stops with the writer who will sign the final paper. The writer retains ultimate responsibility for what the editor drafts, and it is no excuse later that "someone else wrote it for me."

RESTRAINING PRIDE OF AUTHORSHIP

"[F]ierce pride of authorship . . . is, on balance, a good thing," says U.S. Circuit Judge Bruce M. Selya. "It is the pride of the craftsman."[14] Pride of authorship—knowledge that the final writing will carry their name—energizes serious writers to strive for the greatest measure of excellence. Before publication, however, pride unrestrained can weaken the final product by stiffening the writer's resistance to an editor's reasonable suggestions. Economist John Kenneth Galbraith said that "[g]ood writing requires . . . the absence of vanity that allows a man to divorce his writing at least a little from himself."[15]

"[T]he two most crucial aspects" of a writer's character, explains law professor Ira C. Lupu, "are pride and humility. The perfect author has an optimum mix of the two. . . . Of the two qualities, . . . humility is by far the more important."[16]

"Whether or not I like the editor's correction," says Professor Lupu, "I always treat the editorial input as an invitation to revisit a thought or its expression. However frequently I accept an editor's revision, I far more frequently use the proposed revision as a springboard for my own rewrite. Indeed, I try to look at my original sentence, and the editor's proposal, as a self-editor as well as an author. When I can achieve that sort of simultaneous detachment from and proximity to the work, I always come away with a profound sense of improvement in the piece."[17]

Healthy calibration of pride and humility was the most enduring practical writing lesson I learned during my two-year clerkship with Judge Hugh R. Jones of the New York Court of Appeals. In those days before personal computers, the Judge would draft an opinion longhand on a legal pad, and our administrative assistant would type it. Before a draft opinion left the chambers for circulation to the court's other six members, he and his two confidential law clerks would sit at the conference table to parse each paragraph, word for word and line by line.[18]

Collegial parsing extended beyond issues of substance, tone, and persuasion to matters of grammar and syntax. From our first day in chambers, Judge Jones made it clear that the clerks were fellow professionals, colleagues who held his esteem in a collaborative enterprise. He stressed how much he wanted our candid editorial input, and we knew that he meant it. One clerk's concern about something the judge wrote gave him pause, but he also followed a "Rule of Two": Where both clerks expressed similar concern, he considered carefully whether prospective readers might later feel the same way.

Editorial input did not necessarily end with the clerks. Judge Jones also welcomed suggestions from his administrative assistant about spelling, grammar, syntax, and phrasing that caught her trained eye as she typed. The New York Reports never identified her contributions, but the Judge and the clerks knew.

When Judge Jones died in 2001, the *New York Times* praised him as "an intellectual leader of the state's highest court and one of its best writers."[19] A colleague later reminisced that the Judge's "beautifully crafted opinions stand out in the New York Reports as models of scholarship, clarity of thought, and lucid graceful wordsmanship."[20] They were "clear, crisp powerful writings," Chief Judge Judith S. Kaye certified, "not a spare or careless word in them."[21] Accolades such as these demonstrate that Judge Jones had solid reason to be immodest about his writing, but immodesty was not his style.

"[M]y responsibility to the Court as an institution," Judge Jones once wrote, "commands the subordination of my personal interests."[22] By word and deed, the Judge remained true to this responsibility by encouraging editorial give-and-take to help assure that the published reporters would unveil the most polished majority, concurring, or dissenting opinions possible. His openness to editorial contribution served both the Court of Appeals as an institution and the fabric of New York law.

Truth be told, the Judge's reputation for intellect and graceful writing did not depend on editorial input from his law clerks or anyone else. We clerks had some residual impact on an opinion's style and substance, but Judge Jones did not need our editing because he was a consummate writer in his own right. He simply wanted our editing because years in private practice and public service had taught him that anyone's drafts can stand improvement, even a judge's.

THE LEGAL WRITER'S "FAIR HOPE"

Thomas R. Marshall is a name largely lost to American history. His keen observations about the delicate balance between humility and pride of authorship, however, bear recall and reflection.

Marshall was Woodrow Wilson's vice president from 1913 to 1921, during tumultuous times of war and peace. For nearly a year and a half after President Wilson suffered a debilitating stroke shortly after his return from the World War I Versailles Peace Conference in 1919, Marshall stood a fragile heartbeat away from the presidency, uncertain about his role. If the Twenty-Fifth Amendment governing presidential succession (ratified in 1967) had been in effect, Marshall might have become President, or at least Acting President.

Legal writers today can learn from Marshall's insight into the post-war standoff between two personal and political antagonists, the Democratic President Wilson and the Republican Senate leader Henry Cabot Lodge. The President had assumed near unilateral authority to prosecute the war as commander-in-chief, without meaningful participation by Congress. He sought to commit the United States and the world to magnanimity consistent with his January 1917 Peace Without Victory message to the Senate and his Fourteen Points presented to Congress in January 1918.

A keystone of the President's post-war vision was United States entry into the League of Nations, which drew Senator Lodge's steadfast opposition. With neither proud leader prone to compromise, the Senate rejected the Versailles peace treaty and the nation's membership in the League. The United States did not reach a separate peace with Germany (without League membership) until 1921.

"Pride of opinion and authorship, and jealousy of the opinion and authorship of others," wrote Marshall in his memoirs about the post-war standoff, "wreck many a fair hope."[23]

In adversary legal proceedings, a lawyer's "fair hope" is to achieve the most favorable outcome for client or cause. Marshall teaches that a writer's pride of authorship seems counterproductive when it leads the writer to spurn constructive editorial input.

When a writer submerges pride of authorship and carefully weighs an editor's suggestions, the writer focuses attention where it belongs. Early drafts usually disappear in the trash, deleted from the computer, forgotten and never to be seen or heard from again. The audience sees only the published writing, which may survive in law libraries or the public record.

Drawn from the pages of American history, Chapter 9 describes what can happen when a writer's delicate balance of humility and pride of authorship collapses. The chapter tells the story of a proud young lawyer who remained so emotionally invested in his draft that he resented his talented editors for half a century, even though the skillfully edited masterpiece assured the lawyer a revered place in our national heritage and the world's history.

The draft was the Declaration of Independence, and the proud young lawyer was Thomas Jefferson.

---

[1]   Eugene C. Gerhart, Quote It II: A Dictionary of Memorable Legal Quotations 462 (1988) (quoting Justice Brandeis); *Pride of Authorship*, 37 A.B.A. J. 209 (1951) (editorial).

[2]   Ronald C. White, Jr., The Eloquent President: A Portrait of Lincoln Through His Words xx (2005).

[3]   M.J. Hyland, *How to Write Fiction: M.J. Hyland on Revising and Rewriting*, The Guardian (London), Oct. 23, 2011, at 34.

[4]   *Id.*

[5]   Brian Lamb, *Edmund Morris*, in Booknotes: America's Finest Authors on Reading, Writing, and the Power of Ideas 18 (1997).

[6]   Carlos Baker, Hemingway, the Writer as Artist 71 (4th ed. 1972) (quoting Hemingway).

[7]   Writers At Work: The Paris Review Interviews 124 (George Plimpton ed., 2d ed. 1963); *see also, e.g.*, Donald Murray, The Craft of Revision (1991) (quoting John Hersey; "To be a writer is . . . not to be satisfied, to type again, and then again and once more, and over and over.").

[8]   Camille Lamar Campbell, *How to Use a Tube Top and a Dress Code to Demystify the Predictive Writing Process and Build a Framework of Hope During the First Weeks of Class*, 48 Duq. L. Rev. 273, 310 (2010) (quoting Michener).

[9]   Kathryn Ann Lindskoog, Creative Writing for People Who Can't Not Write 62 (1989) (quoting Michener); *see also, e.g.*, Robert Van Gelder, *An Interview With Mr. E. B. White, Essayist*, N.Y. Times, Aug. 2, 1942, at BR2 (quoting White: "I rewrite a good deal to make it clear."); John Irving, *Trying to Save Piggy Sneed, N.Y. Times*, Aug. 22, 1982, sec. 7, at BR 3 ("Half my life is an act of revision; more than half the act is performed with small changes.").

[10]   Judith Frutig, *Dr. Seuss's Green-Eggs-and-Ham World*, Christian Sci. Monitor, May 12, 1978.

[11]   Michael D'Antonio, *Sneer When You Say 'Journalist'*, L.A. Times, Aug. 24, 2003, Pt. 9, at 20 (quoting Singer).

[12]   *Loveable Old Volcano*, Time, Mar. 6, 1950, at 72, 77 (quoting Ross).

[13]   George D. Gopen, Writing From a Legal Perspective 1 (West 1981).

[14]   Bruce M. Selya, *In Search of Less*, 74 Tex. L. Rev. 1277, 1279 (1996).

[15]   John Kenneth Galbraith, A View from the Stands: Of People, Politics, Military Power and the Arts 386 (Andrea D. Williams ed. 1986).

[16]   Ira C. Lupu, *Six Authors In Search of a Character*, 70 Chi.-Kent L. Rev. 71, 73–74 (1994).

[17]   *Id.* at 74.

[18]   Douglas E. Abrams, *Judges and Their Editors*, 3 Alb. Gov't L. Rev. 392 (2010); Douglas E. Abrams, *Hugh Richard Jones*, in The Judges of the New York Court of Appeals: A Biographical History 725 (Albert M. Rosenblatt ed., 2007).

[19]   Laura Mansnerus, *Hugh R. Jones, 86, Ex-Judge On New York Court of Appeals*, N.Y. Times, Mar. 6, 2001, at A19.

[20]   Stewart F. Hancock, Jr., *Meeting the Needs: Fairness, Morality, Creativity and Common Sense*, 68 Alb. L. Rev. 81, 81 (2004).

[21]   John Caher, *Judge Hugh R. Jones*, N.Y.L.J., Mar. 6, 2001, at 2 (obituary) (one of the Court's "best writers"); Judith S. Kaye, *A Tribute to the Honorable Hugh R. Jones*, 65 Alb. L. Rev. 1, 2 (2001).

[22] Hugh R. Jones, *Cogitations on Appellate Decision-Making*, 34 Rec. Ass'n Bar City of N.Y., 543, 545 (1979), *reprinted in* 52 N.Y. St. B.J. 189, 190 (Apr. 1980).

[23] Thomas R. Marshall, Recollections of Thomas R. Marshall, Vice-President and Hoosier Philosopher: A Hoosier Salad 363–64 (1925).

CHAPTER 9

THE DECLARATION OF INDEPENDENCE: PRIDE OF AUTHORSHIP UNRESTRAINED

■ ■ ■

In June of 1776, more than a year had passed since the Battle of Lexington and Concord ignited the American Revolution. An epic struggle loomed against the greatest military power on Earth, and the Second Continental Congress sensed that nationhood would depend on written reason and passion, and not only on the force of arms.

On Congress' behalf, one of its members, 33-year-old Virginia lawyer Thomas Jefferson, drafted the Declaration of Independence. For the next half century, Jefferson's fierce pride of authorship, unrestrained by humility, kept him from crediting Congress for skilled editing that helped make him a national icon by sharpening his powerful, but less than thoroughly polished, draft. From the story of lawyer Jefferson's lingering bitterness, lawyers today can better respect cooperative editors as allies, not adversaries, in the joint pursuit of effective writing.

"YOU CAN WRITE TEN TIMES BETTER THAN I CAN"

To draft the Declaration of Independence that would later reverberate throughout the 13 colonies and the world, Congress appointed from its ranks a Committee of Five on June 11, 1776. The appointees were Benjamin Franklin, John Adams, Robert Livingston, Roger Sherman, and Jefferson, Congress' youngest delegate.

Because Franklin was lame from severe gout, and because Livingston and Sherman held no special gifts for the eloquence that the hour demanded, the committee assigned Adams and Jefferson to produce a draft. Adams proposed that Jefferson write alone, reportedly citing the Virginian's rhetorical skills and explaining, "You can write ten times better than I can."[1]

Like other gifted writers, Jefferson knew the audience. The moment called for an evocative appeal to the colonists' hearts and minds, and to the sensibilities of European powers that might intervene on the colonists' side, as France did in 1778. Few readers would share Jefferson's knowledge of political philosophy, and fewer still would pursue this knowledge as war loomed. Jefferson said that he would "place before mankind the common sense of the subject in terms so plain and firm as to command their assent."[2]

Writing in the second floor parlor of a Philadelphia home, Jefferson summoned extant political philosophy, added his own ideas, and presented his draft Declaration to the Committee of Five within a few days. "After decades as a writer and editor," reports Franklin biographer H.W. Brands, "Franklin knew good prose when he read it. He treated Jefferson's draft gently."[3] The committee preserved the draft intact except for about two dozen relatively minor edits, though one memorable line changed. Jefferson had written, "We hold these truths to be sacred and undeniable." For the last three words, either Jefferson himself or Franklin substituted the more concise, simpler "We hold these truths to be self-evident."[4]

REVISION AND RESENTMENT

Beginning on July 2, the full 65-member Congress convened in the Pennsylvania State House in Philadelphia and parsed Jefferson's draft for nearly two and a half days. Historians have praised the young Virginian as "a genius with language"[5] whose draft Declaration resonated with "rolling cadences and mellifluous phrases, soaring in their poetry and powerful despite their polish."[6] But Jefferson's congressional colleagues faced serious work because, according to historian Pauline Maier, the draft "revealed both splendid artistry and signs of haste."[7]

Most of the approximately 80 changes Congress made to the draft Declaration enhanced its persuasive force. Jefferson, for example, alleged that the King had "suffered the administration of justice totally to cease in some of these states." Congress chose conciseness, precision, simplicity, and clarity: "He has obstructed the administration of justice."[8]

Congress also aroused Jefferson's lifelong resentment by deleting a few passages that the Committee of Five had accepted a week earlier. One deleted passage (later denounced as a "vituperative, turgid and unfair indictment" by one historian, and as "patently false" by another) blamed the King for the slave trade, perhaps to salve Jefferson's own conscience as a slaveholder torn by the inhumanity of bondage.[9] Another deletion displaced reason with passion before closing with a plea that "[w]e might have been a free and great people together."[10]

Watching Congress excise about a quarter of the draft, including a few rambling clauses and sentences, was painful for Jefferson, who, according to historian Page Smith, suffered from "almost pathological sensitivity."[11] Watching his draft run the congressional gauntlet so disturbed Jefferson that the elder statesman Franklin, sitting with him during the proceedings, tried unsuccessfully to soothe the dispirited Virginian's wounded pride by gently explaining the dynamics of a deliberative body.

Franklin left the conversation unable to overcome the hurt for what Jefferson viewed as mutilations of his work.[12]

Historian Maier called Congress' parsing of Jefferson's draft "an act of group editing that has to be one of the great marvels of history."[13] "This was no hack editing job," she continued, because "the delegates who labored over the draft Declaration had a splendid ear for language. . . . By exercising their intelligence, political good sense, and a discerning sense of language, the delegates managed to make the Declaration at once more accurate and more consonant with the convictions of their constituents, and to enhance both its power and its eloquence."[14]

Jefferson nonetheless remained resentful in letters to friends shortly after Congress approved the edited Declaration on July 4, 1776 and prepared it for publication. When he published his autobiography in 1821, the 77-year-old Jefferson continued to disparage congressional editing of his draft. Explaining that "[t]he sentiments of men are known not only by what they receive but what they reject also," he presented his entire Declaration "as originally reported," and underlined "the parts struck out by Congress."[15] He died five years later, still content to let Americans decide for themselves.

THE VERDICT OF HISTORY

Historians recognize the Declaration of Independence as "the most lyrical and memorable statement of American values,"[16] indeed as "the most cherished document in American history."[17] When President Lincoln at Gettysburg in 1863 told the nation that "[f]our score and seven years ago our fathers brought forth on this continent, a new nation," he counted from the Declaration in 1776, and not from the Constitution's ratification little more than a decade later.

Lincoln called the Declaration an "immortal emblem of humanity."[18] Justice Robert H. Jackson praised it for producing, in "majestic cadence" and "plain words," "the boldest, the noblest, and best known of all American writings."[19] President Dwight D. Eisenhower called the Declaration "a charter of human liberty and dignity."[20] President George H.W. Bush called it "a beacon for people all over the world seeking freedom."[21]

In his Second Inaugural address, President Obama echoed these earlier sentiments: "What makes us exceptional—what makes us American—is our allegiance to an idea articulated in a declaration made more than two centuries ago. . . . Today we continue a never-ending journey to bridge the meaning of those words with the realities of our time."[22]

As they sustain working relationships with their own editors, today's legal writers should recall that Jefferson's congressional editors deserve a share of the credit for shaping the Declaration of Independence. Historian

Carl L. Becker delivered the generally accepted verdict: "Congress left the Declaration better than it found it" by crafting a living document that was "brief, free of verbiage, a model of clear, concise, and simple statement."[23]

Jefferson and Adams both died on the afternoon of July 4, 1826, at nearly the hour when Congress had announced the Declaration of Independence exactly 50 years earlier. In his long lifetime, the Sage of Monticello could have drawn greater satisfaction from his immortal achievement if he had viewed his legislative editors as valuable resources rather than troublesome meddlers. Pride of authorship, the engine that drives committed writers toward excellence, is best reserved for the final document, and not for the preliminary drafts that shape it.

"WHEN THOMAS JEFFERSON DINED ALONE"

On April 29, 1962, President John F. Kennedy and his wife Jacqueline hosted a formal White House dinner honoring the Western Hemisphere's 49 living Nobel Prize laureates. "I think," he toasted the luminaries, "this is the most extraordinary collection of talent, of human knowledge, that has ever been gathered together at the White House, with the possible exception of when Thomas Jefferson dined alone."[24]

More than two centuries after it helped launch the American experience, the Declaration of Independence remains Jefferson's written gift to the nation. Growth and change have marked the history of the Republic since 1776, but lawyer Jefferson's lofty place among American writers remains—with help from his editors.

---

[1]   David McCullough, John Adams 119 (2001).

[2]   Thomas Fleming, The Man From Monticello: An Intimate Life of Thomas Jefferson 53 (1969).

[3]   H.W. Brands, The First American: The Life and Times of Benjamin Franklin 511 (2000).

[4]   Carl L. Becker, The Declaration of Independence: A Study In the History of Political Ideas 142 (1942); *id.* at 141–71 (drafts showing the Committee's edits); Dumas Malone, 1 Jefferson and His Time: Jefferson the Virginian 221 (1948).

[5]   Joseph J. Ellis, American Creation: Triumphs and Tragedies At the Founding of the Republic 56 (2008).

[6]   Walter Isaacson, Benjamin Franklin: An American Life 311 (2003).

[7]   Pauline Maier, American Scripture 99 (1997).

[8]   David McCullough, *supra* note 1 at 134.

[9]   Robert Leckie, George Washington's War: The Saga of the American Revolution 255 (1992) ("vituperative," etc.); Gary B. Nash, The Unknown American Revolution: The Unruly Birth of Democracy and the Struggle to Create America 208 (2005) ("patently false").

[10]   David McCullough, *supra* note 1 at 134–35.

[11]   Page Smith, Jefferson: A Revealing Biography 102 (1976); *see also* Carl L. Becker, *supra* note 4 at 174–84 (showing Congress' edits).

[12]   H.W. Brands, *supra* note 3 at 511–12.

[13]   Pauline Maier, *supra* note 7 at 98; *see generally id.*, ch. 3 (1997) ("Mr. Jefferson and His Editors").

[14]   *Id.* at 148, 150.

[15]   Thomas Jefferson, *Autobiography*, The Avalon Project, http://avalon.law.yale.edu/19th_century/jeffauto.asp (visited Aug. 11, 2020).

[16]   Joseph J. Ellis, *supra* note 5 at 234.

[17]   Noble E. Cunningham, Jr., In Pursuit of Reason: The Life of Thomas Jefferson 51 (1987).

[18]   Charles Sumner, A Memorial of Abraham Lincoln, Late President of the United States 110 (1865).

[19]   Robert H. Jackson, *Independence Day Address*, July 4, 1941.

[20]   Dwight D. Eisenhower, *Radio and Television Report to the American People on the European Trip* (Sept. 10, 1959), https://www.presidency.ucsb.edu/documents/radio-and-television-report-the-american-people-the-european-trip (visited Aug. 11, 2020).

[21]   States News Serv., *Able Accounts: Building Upon the Promise of the Americans With Disabilities Act*, July 27, 2020.

[22]   *Inaugural Address by President Barack Obama*, https://obamawhitehouse.archives.gov/the-press-office/2013/01/21/inaugural-address-president-barack-obama (Jan. 21, 2013).

[23]   Carl L. Becker, *supra* note 4 at 209.

[24]   Public Papers of the Presidents of the United States: John F. Kennedy, 1962, No. 161, at 347 (1963).

CHAPTER 10

PROOFREADING

■ ■ ■

"Proof read carefully to see if you any words out," advised writer William Safire, tongue-in-cheek.[1] "If you reread your work," he added lightly, "you can find on rereading that a great deal of repetition can be avoided by rereading and editing."[2]

Chapters 8 and 9 emphasized substantive editing by the writer and third persons; this chapter presents guidelines for writers and editors as they proofread for such shortcomings as typographical errors, misspellings, grammatical mistakes, incorrect citations, and the writer's undeleted bracketed reminders. Chapter 8 made the point that editors may simultaneously perform proofreading and substantive review.

The writer's own proofreading comes first because lawyers bear ultimate responsibility for the writings they sign. But at some point, even talented writers hit the proverbial "brick wall" and third-person proofreading becomes essential. In a law firm of any size, a lawyer may enlist proofreaders from among partners, associates, paralegals, or student law clerks. Solo practitioners can usually enlist proofreaders from among some members of this array.

"[P]erfection is an impossibility" in any endeavor, legendary UCLA basketball coach John Wooden taught his players, but "*striving* for perfection is not. . . . Do the best you can under the conditions that exist."[3] For lawyers during the proofreading process, these conditions frequently include impending deadlines, obligations to various clients, and heavy caseloads. An occasional typographical error or other misstep can elude even careful proofreading by writer and editor, but striving for error-free writing remains a bare minimum expected from law students and lawyers.

PROOFREADING GUIDELINES FOR LAWYERS

Even if readers can figure out what the lawyer means to say, proofreading lapses can raise doubts about whether the lawyer's research and argument reflect similar carelessness. Even an occasional lapse can arouse unwelcome notice because readers characteristically take flawless professional writing for granted until flaws appear. These guidelines help shape proofreading by lawyers and their editors:

1. *Heed floors, but reach for ceilings.* Court rules typically regulate such matters as a submission's font size, line spacing, and margins. A lawyer who runs afoul of these rules risks having the court impose a sanction such as striking the submission or ordering a monetary penalty.

Court rules do not deliver the last word, however, because they leave the writer, and the editor or proofreader, much room to fashion a submission that appears pleasing enough to the eyes to make people want to read it. "Presentation is as important as substance," Professor S.I. Strong advises students about the likely reactions of future employers, opponents, and clients.[4] For example, shorter paragraphs that maintain coherence (perhaps no more than half a page, sometimes shorter) make life easier for readers, but paragraph length remains unregulated by court rule.

2. *Cite-check carefully.* The lawyer should assume that readers will check each cited authority for accuracy, content, and meaning. Readers often do not go this far, but the writer never knows which cites may attract close attention. When parties' rights and obligations hang in the balance, every citation is fair game to a reader who seeks to verify, challenge, or even satisfy curiosity.

Persuasion depends on winning and holding readers' confidence, and providing incorrect or incomplete cites is a quick way to forfeit this confidence by leading readers to question whether the lawyer also has cut corners with research, analysis, or argument.

Until recently, citing to the wrong volume or page, or misspelling an authority, often consigned readers to time-consuming, frustrating, and sometimes fruitless searches through reporters or other printed sources. Verifying a quote required fishing for the proper volume on the library shelf and thumbing through the pages, sometimes line by line. Today electronic word searches can often locate mis-cited sources quickly, but without necessarily dispelling readers' doubts about the writer or the argument.

3. *Follow approved citation form.* Law depends on rules, and courts may resent having to recast skimpy citations to conform to the rules recited in *The Bluebook: A Uniform System of Citation*, the *ALWD Guide to Legal Citation*, or whatever style the court requires.[5] The court knows its own citation conventions and expects counsel to heed them.

4. *Avoid providing citations for nearly every proposition, even ones that need no citations.* In early 1L Legal Research and Writing assignments, professors may instruct students learning the ropes to provide citations for straightforward propositions that in law practice need no articulated support.

I advise 1Ls that the writing process changes with law school graduation, or even before. A gaggle of unnecessary citations slows the presentation, and may lead readers to wonder whether the lawyer really grasps the essence of the argument. When the lawyer appears to lack self-confidence, readers may lose confidence in the lawyer before long.

5. *Beware of "spell-check" and similar technologies.* Similar to many other contemporary "labor saving" devices, spell-check is not everything it first seems. A federal district court recently criticized the plaintiff's counsel for submitting a brief with gaffes that overlooked the porous nature of this software. "Spellcheck," the court's opinion cautioned, "ensures that what is written is an English word; it does not check for whether it is the word the writer intended."[6]

The district court's antidote? "[S]pellcheck is no substitute for proofreading."[7] As if to underscore this message, another judge recalls a case concerning a paramour, whom a party's submitted but evidently unproofed brief called a "power mower" throughout.[8]

Spell-check alerts me to problems as I type. Near the end of a project, I sometimes pay closer attention to spell-check as I do my own proofreading. Spell-check, however, is a tool and not a crutch, valuable but not a short-cut for old-fashioned proofreading. Writers and proofreaders should pay close attention to the printed page and keep a dictionary nearby or online.

6. *Spell names correctly.* Knowing the audience (discussed in Chapter 2) means correctly spelling its members' names, and the names of any organization with which they are affiliated. This injunction may seem simple, but names matter and errors stand out from the page. Errors may escape detection when proofreading keys on "the law," or when the writer gets careless with a form cut-and-pasted from a prior matter.

Professor Louis Lusky, who joined Columbia Law School's faculty after a versatile career in practice, would tell his students that the surest way to lose a client is to misspell the client's name in a court submission or other written communication. Similarly disconcerting is misspelling the name of someone the lawyer asks to do the client a favor, or the name of a judge the lawyer seeks to persuade.

7. *Exercise care with electronic submissions.* Technology provides no excuse for relaxing the care that was required when lawyers mailed or hand-delivered their papers to the courthouse and the other parties. For busy lawyers, it is too easy sometimes to hit a computer key prematurely and then suffer "sender's remorse" after it is too late.

8. *Follow a "4:00 Rule."* The time of day may matter to careful writers. I am a "morning person," and I prefer to proofread (and indeed, to write) in the early hours. Other writers may feel more creative later in the day.

But regardless of personal preference during the writing process itself, writers can avoid last-minute embarrassment by heeding a "4:00 Rule" on completion. Unless a deadline or similar obligation demands immediacy, lawyers should resist sending a brief or other writing after 4:00 in the afternoon, near the end of a long day. I even resist sending personal correspondence after that hour.

In the absence of an unyielding immediate deadline, anything that recipients can do with a brief or other writing sent after 4:00, they can usually do with the writing sent first thing the next morning. Writers can benefit from taking even a swift look at substance and style before dispatching the final product after a night's sleep.

9. *Remain open to proofreading innovations.* Chief Justice Earl Warren explained why he followed the unorthodox practice of reading daily newspapers from back to front: "I always turn to the sports page first," he said. "The sports page records people's accomplishments; the front page, nothing but man's failure."[9]

Some writing professionals recommend that writer and editor proofread a document from back to front because reading each sentence out of context spotlights "failures" that, camouflaged by the argument's flow, might otherwise escape even trained eyes.[10] The recommendation warrants consideration from thoughtful writers.

Continuing a creative oral process that (as described in Chapter 2) can enhance early drafts, some writing professionals also counsel proofreading aloud for substance, style, and inadvertent miscues.[11] At any stage of a writing's gestation, vocalizing enlists not only the eyes, but also the ears. The more senses at work, the better.

CRITICISM, SANCTIONS, AND REDUCED FEE AWARDS

As advocates strive to fulfill their professional obligation to deliver briefs and other submissions marked by careful proofreading, courts have reason to accept occasional proofreading miscues. Generally former practitioners themselves, judges can understand that advocates in the public and private sectors frequently write under time pressures more stringent than those typically imposed on judges themselves. One federal district court stated the test this way: "While an occasional typo is perhaps inevitable and certainly forgivable, an abundance of errors tends to discredit the substance of a brief."[12]

An abundance of errors, explains another federal court, is a "disservice to the court, and more importantly to the client."[13] The client can suffer when the lawyer's subpar writing undermines the court's confidence in the soundness of the advocacy itself. Suspicion may arise that a writer who is less than competent in one may be less than competent in the other.

A submission with errors whose numbers cross the line from occasional to abundant can lead to court imposition of sanctions or to other adverse professional consequences. For one thing, the court's opinion may publicly criticize the lawyer's brief or other filing. In extreme cases, opinions have labeled error-riddled briefs with such pejoratives as "slipshod,"[14] "sloppy,"[15] "careless,"[16] and "poorly written."[17]

In one decision, the U.S. Court of Appeals for the Fifth Circuit said this in its published opinion: "Usually we do not comment on technical and grammatical errors, because anyone can make such an occasional mistake, but here the miscues are so egregious and obvious that an average fourth grader would have avoided most of them."[18]

Even when the court's opinion does not identify the lawyer by name, readers encountering a pejorative can readily determine the lawyer's identity from the list of appearances that follow the case's caption.

A LAWYER'S VALUABLE ASSET

Even without criticism or other judicial sanction, proofreading deficiencies can stain a lawyer's personal and professional reputation. In many private-law matters, the immediate audience for a lawyer's brief or other submission may not extend beyond the court, parties, counsel, and clients. Even where written submissions become public records, proofreading deficiencies may go largely unnoticed outside this small circle of readers.

Lawyers, however, cannot count on such confinement. In cities, suburbs, and outstate areas alike, the bar often reduces itself to a relatively discrete group bound by personal relationships, word of mouth, and experiences developed over time. The specialization that characterizes contemporary law practice may constrict the circle still further. Sooner or later, word gets around.

A track record of sub-par filings can encourage opposing lawyers to seek to take advantage, and can encourage courts to lose confidence in the lawyer's advocacy. Proofreading stumbles can cast doubt among other bar members and prior clients who might contemplate new relationships with the lawyer, including whether to send referrals.

Reputation for competence, like reputation for integrity, is a lawyer's valuable asset. A lawyer's reputation, wrote Chief Judge Benjamin N. Cardozo when he sat on the New York Court of Appeals, "is a plant of tender growth, and its bloom, once lost, is not easily restored."[19] Benjamin Franklin taught more pointedly that, "[i]t takes many good deeds to build a good reputation, and only one bad one to lose it."[20]

[1]   *William Safire's Rules for Writers*, Univ. of Glasgow, http://www.chem.gla.ac.uk/ research/groups/protein/pert/safire.rules.html (visited Sept. 20, 2020).

[2]   *Id.*

[3]   John Wooden, Wooden: A Lifetime of Observations and Reflections On and Off the Court 29 (1997) (emphasis in original).

[4]   S.I. Strong, How to Write Law Essays and Exams 130 (2006).

[5]   The Bluebook: A Uniform System of Citation (21st ed. 2020); Ass'n of Legal Writing Dirs. & Coleen M. Barger, ALWD Guide to Legal Citation (6th ed. 2017).

[6]   Ott v. H & M Hennes & Mauritz LP, No. 14-CV-556, 2019 WL 6393821, at *5 (E.D. Wis. Oct. 22, 2015).

[7]   *Id.*

[8]   Fred Horlbeck, *S.C. Supreme Court Justice Kaye G. Hearn Gives Pointers On What Advocates Should and Shouldn't Say and Write*, S.C. Lawyers Weekly, Dec. 17, 2010 (quoting Justice Hearn).

[9]   *See* Alec Lewis, The Quotable Quotations Book 262 (1980) (quoting Chief Justice Warren).

[10]   *E.g.*, Joyce Rosenberg, *Spell Check Is Not Your Friend (and Other Tips for Effective Proofreading)*, J. Kan. Bar Ass'n 11 (Apr. 2012); Scott Moise, *Glass Houses: Proofreading*, 19 S.C. Law. 44, 45 (July 2007).

[11]   *See, e.g.*, Jim McElhaney, *Style Matters: Write Briefs As If They Could Win Your Case- Because They Can*, 94 A.B.A. J. 28 (June 2008).

[12]   Gaskins v. Baltimore City Public Schools, No. JKB-15-2961, 2016 WL 192535, at *3 (D. Md. Jan. 15, 2016), *aff'd sub nom.* Gaskins v. Abiodun, 649 F. App'x 307 (4th Cir. 2016).

[13]   Ott, *supra* note 6, at *5.

[14]   Gandy v. Lynx Credit, No. 3:14-CV-0369-B, 2014 WL 6805501, at *1 n.2 (N.D. Tex. Dec. 3, 2014).

[15]   Poulter v. Cottrell, Inc., No. 12-CV-1071, 2016 WL 7451630, at *1 n.2 (N.D. Ill. Dec. 28, 2016).

[16]   Holmes v. Shulkin, No. 16-0099, 2017 WL 40790027, at *2 n.1 (Ct. Vet. App. Sept. 15, 2017).

[17]   Ayala v. Armstrong, No.1:16-cv-00501, 2019 WL 96299, at *1 (D. Idaho Jan. 3, 2010).

[18]   Sanches v. Carrollton-Farmers Branch Ind. Sch. Dist., 647 F.3d 156, 172 n.13 (5th Cir. 2011). *See also, e.g.*, Timmons v. Lockheed Martin Corp., No. 11-cv-03408, 2013 WL 24667705, at *3 n.4 (D. Colo. June 7, 2013) ("[T]he pleading submitted by counsel for [the plaintiff] is one of the most shoddily drafted the Court has ever seen.").

[19]   People ex rel. Karlin v. Culkin, 162 N.E. 487, 492 (N.Y. 1928).

[20]   Joseph Lieberman, *Recovery and Reinvestment Spending: Implementing a Bold Oversight Strategy*, S. Homeland Security and Gov'tal Affairs Comm. 1, 1 (Apr. 2, 2009), http:// www.hsgac.senate.gov/download/040209jilopen (visited Jan. 30, 2016).

PART 5

DISMANTLING BARRIERS

■ ■ ■

"Writing is talking to someone else on paper," said William Zinsser.[1] Chapter 2 summoned lawyers to Earn the Right to a Reader. A legal writer earns the best opportunity to reach and persuade readers when the writer maintains clear lines of communication.

Dismantling barriers to effective communication has been a recurrent theme of this book because good legal writing begins with concise, precise, simple, and clear expression. Part Five focuses on three specific barriers— jargon, acronyms, and footnotes. Each may hold a place in good legal writing, but each also remains prone to misuse that can stymie otherwise effective expression.

---

[1]   William Zinsser, On Writing Well x (2001).

CHAPTER 11

JARGON

■ ■ ■

The Merriam-Webster Dictionary defines "jargon" as "confused unintelligible language; . . . the technical terminology or characteristic idiom of a special activity or group."[1] Jargon may help a legal writer communicate with an audience that consists entirely of lawyers who are trained in the field that the writer addresses. Chapter 2 explains, for example, why a tort lawyer's use of undefined jargon such as the term "causation" may resonate with an audience of tort lawyers but not with an audience of laypersons, or even of other lawyers. Joined by common professional experience, the tort lawyers share a "special activity or group."

In the absence of this common professional experience, however, undefined legal jargon such as "causation" can cloud presentations of law or fact when readers know less, and perhaps much less, than the writer. Unless the writer bridges the knowledge gap by explaining the term or by presenting a legally accurate plain English discussion, this cloudiness demonstrates what Merriam-Webster calls "confused unintelligible language."

Chapter 6's discussion of George Orwell's classic essay on writing links foreign words or phrases with jargon. But legal jargon also includes words or phrases (foreign or otherwise) whose meaning is likely to be readily understood only by readers who belong to a group that is versed in the field of law that the lawyer writes about. Outside this group may be a judge who will decide the case that the lawyer briefs.

"INTO EVERYDAY ENGLISH"

An example from the courtroom describes the avoidable barriers that jargon can impose between brief writer and judge. In *Indiana Lumbermens Mutual Insurance Co. v. Reinsurance Results, Inc.* (2008), the U.S. Court of Appeals for the Seventh Circuit held that the parties' contract did not require the plaintiff insurer to pay commissions to the company it had retained to review the insurer's reinsurance claims.[2] Writing for the panel, Judge Posner reported that the parties' briefs "were difficult for us judges to understand because of the density of the reinsurance jargon in them."[3]

"There is nothing wrong with a specialized vocabulary—for use by specialists," Judge Posner explained for the panel. "Federal district and circuit judges, however, ... are generalists. We hear very few cases involving reinsurance, and cannot possibly achieve expertise in reinsurance practices except by the happenstance of having practiced in that area before becoming a judge.... Lawyers should understand the judges' limited knowledge of specialized fields and choose their vocabulary accordingly. Every esoteric term used by the reinsurance industry has a counterpart in ordinary English."[4]

Judge Posner concluded that counsel "could have saved us some work and presented their positions more effectively had they done the translations from reinsurancese into everyday English themselves."[5]

"QUAKING QUAGMIRES"

Jargon's capacity to perplex the federal and state bench is not new, nor is this capacity limited to reinsurance or any other particular field of law. In 1953, for example, Dean William L. Prosser wrote about another perplexing field: "[T]he realm of the conflicts of laws is a dismal swamp, filled with quaking quagmires, and inhabited by learned but eccentric professors who theorize about mysterious matters in strange and incomprehensible jargon. The ordinary court . . . is quite lost when engulfed and entangled in it."[6]

A federal or state court can find itself "quite lost" amid jargon today because, as American law has grown increasingly intricate in recent decades, lawyers have gravitated toward specialty practices. Specialization means that judges tend to come from private sector or public sector practices that exposed them regularly to only some of the federal and state substantive law that determines cases that now fill their dockets. Few lawyers practice civil and criminal law simultaneously, and the sheer breadth of constitutional, statutory, and administrative intricacies often creates doctrines most familiar to specialists.

Trial and appellate judges candidly acknowledge their dependence on counsel to help them navigate through what Dean Prosser called "strange and incomprehensible jargon."[7] "Dropping a judge in the middle of an alien landscape without a map and expecting him to get his bearings from fragments of testimony couched in occupational jargon to which he has not previously been exposed," explains one federal district court, "is not conducive to informed decisionmaking."[8] Nor are alien landscapes conducive to effective lawyering because they can diminish the client's power of persuasion.

WHAT READERS KNOW

Judges are not the only audience that legal jargon can baffle. Justice Elena Kagan challenges legal writers generally to "figure out how to communicate complicated ideas to people who know a lot less than you do about a certain subject."[9] "Figuring out" means weighing careful use of jargon for readers who can understand it, but also sensing when to spurn jargon for readers who cannot. The latter category may number not only judges, but also such other people as clients, opposing parties and counsel, and sometimes members of the general public.

University of Alabama football coach Paul "Bear" Bryant used to say that "[n]o coach has ever won a game by what he knows; it's what his players know that counts."[10] The client similarly stands a better chance of prevailing based not on what its lawyer knows, but on what the lawyer wants readers know once they finish the lawyer's writing. If the lawyer senses beforehand that jargon may confound the audience, the jargon probably will. When in doubt, leave it out. Opt for what Judge Posner calls "a counterpart in ordinary English."

[1] *Jargon*, Merriam-Webster, http://www.merriam-webster.com/dictionary/jargon (visited Aug. 14, 2020).

[2] 513 F.3d 652, 658 (7th Cir. 2008).

[3] *Id.*

[4] *Id.*

[5] *Id. See also, e.g.*, Filarsky v. Life Ins. Co. of N. Am, 391 F. Supp. 3d 928, 930 n.1 (N.D. Cal. 2019) ("the parties' briefs were each replete with undefined medical jargon . . ., making the briefing rather difficult to review and . . . creating extra work for the Court").

[6] William L. Prosser, *Interstate Publication*, 51 Mich. L. Rev. 959, 971 (1953).

[7] Shoshone-Bannock Tribes of Fort Hall Reservation v. Shalala, 988 F. Supp. 1306, 1318 (D. Or. 1997), *reconsidered*, 999 F. Supp. 1395 (D. Or. 1998). *See also* Rabin v. Concord Assets Group, Inc., No. 89 Civ. 6130, 1995 WL 645441, at *6 (S.D.N.Y. Nov. 2, 1995).

[8] Langston v. Illinois Bell Telep. Co., No. 88 C 3578, 1990 WL 129567, at *6 n.8 (N.D. Ill. Sept. 3, 1990).

[9] Robert Barnes, *Kagan Made Her Mark in a Bold Rookie Term*, Wash. Post, Sept. 26, 2011, at A1 (quoting Justice Kagan).

[10] Paul "Bear" Bryant, http://www.quotes-positive.com/quote/no-coach-ever-game-knows-101/ (visited Aug. 14, 2020).

CHAPTER 12

ACRONYMS

■ ■ ■

According to Merriam-Webster's Dictionary, an acronym is "a word formed from the initial letter or letters of each of the successive parts or major parts of a compound term."[1] Well-known examples include ABA and AMA—the American Bar Association and the American Medical Association.

Similar to misuse of jargon, misuse of acronyms may confound judges or other readers. Misuse assumed center stage in 2012, when the U.S. Court of Appeals for the District of Columbia Circuit decided *National Association of Regulatory Utility Commissioners v. United States Department of Energy*.[2] The three-judge panel held that the challenged agency determination violated the Nuclear Waste Policy Act of 1982.[3]

The parties' briefs had ladled hefty servings of acronym-filled alphabet soup. The Association argued, for example, that, "[a]lthough DOE has not disclaimed its obligation to dispose of SNF, it is undisputed that DOE currently has no active waste disposal program. . . . The BRC is undertaking none of the waste disposal program activities identified in NWPA § 302(d). Its existence therefore cannot justify continued NWF fee collection."[4]

The agency's brief countered that "[t]he plain language of the NWPA . . . provides the Secretary [of Energy] with broad discretion in determining whether to recommend a change to the statutory NWF fee. . . . In section 302(a)(2) of the NWPA, Congress set the amount of the NWF fee—which is paid only by utilities that enter into contracts with DOE for the disposal of their SNF and HLW."[5]

The unanimous D.C. Circuit panel admonished the parties for "littering their briefs," and for "abandon[ing] any attempt to write in plain English, instead abbreviating every conceivable agency and statute involved, whether familiar or not."[6] The panel quoted from the Circuit's *Handbook of Practice and Internal Procedures*: "[P]arties are strongly urged to limit the use of acronyms. While acronyms may be used for entities and statutes with widely recognized initials, such as FERC and FOIA, parties should avoid using acronyms that are not widely known."[7]

"LOUSY BRIEF WRITING"

In 2013, the D.C. Circuit rejected a few briefs for ignoring the handbook's directive. The matter came to a head in that court again the next year, when *Delaware Riverkeeper Network, Inc. v. Federal Energy Regulatory Commission* struck down the agency's approval of a natural gas pipeline project.[8] Two concurring judges joined the court's decision on the merits, but chastised the petitioner for larding its brief with obscure acronyms.[9] Pulling no punches, the two judges said that "the practice constitutes lousy brief writing."[10]

Outside the D.C. Circuit, some courts try their best to guess the meaning of unfamiliar acronyms undefined by a party's brief.[11] Some courts proceed as best they can without definition.[12] Other courts do their own research to divine meaning.[13] Still other courts simply leave undecided a question that turns on a mystifying acronym.[14]

Sometimes the author of a brief or other writing appends a glossary defining acronyms used, but glossaries provide only partial cures at best. "Even with a glossary, a judge finds himself or herself constantly looking back to recall what an acronym means," said the D.C. Circuit in *Delaware Riverkeeper Network.*[15] "Perhaps not surprisingly, we never see that in a brief filed by well-skilled appellate specialists. It has been almost a marker, dividing the better lawyers from the rest."[16]

In 2020, the D.C. Circuit continued to caution parties to exercise self-restraint in their use of acronyms. In *M.M.V. v. Barr,*[17] the panel's order set a briefing schedule and reiterated the message from the Circuit's *Handbook of Practice and Internal Procedures.*[18]

Writers contemplating acronyms can stay on the safe side of the marker by heeding two guidelines of effective writing that Chapters 2 and 6 presented—Know the Audience, and Apply a Rule of Reason.

KNOW THE AUDIENCE

The confusion that acronyms created in the 2012 Nuclear Waste Policy Act case seemed especially stark because the D.C. Circuit panel's three judges were not newcomers to the federal administrative thicket. The court's docket is steeped in federal administrative law. The court's federal agency-review proceedings include ones involving the Department of Energy, and the judges who heard the Nuclear Waste Policy Act appeal had served an aggregate of 59 years on the court.[19]

The practical upshot of administrative complexity, according to the U.S. Court of Appeals for the Fifth Circuit, is that lawyers regularly immersed in an agency's practice may acquire experience that judges simply do not have, regardless of the judges' own backgrounds before or after ascending to the bench.[20] Inside or outside the administrative sphere, according to one federal district court, lawyers' casual use of concocted acronyms brings risks that arise whenever legal writers "presuppose specialized knowledge on the part of their readers."[21] "It is the responsibilities of the parties to properly educate the court," explained a federal district judge.[22] Unrestrained use of acronyms impedes the educative process.

Knowing the audience also means knowing the court, including its published rules. Once the D.C. Circuit handbook sternly flagged acronym abuse and the court underscored this abuse in a published opinion, future parties had no excuse to resume business as usual.

APPLY A RULE OF REASON

Enter Chapter 6's Rule of Reason. On the one hand, when a lawyer writes for a relatively small audience of specialists or fully identifies a generally known acronym in the early pages, the acronym can simplify the writer's message and help readers proceed more smoothly. Using some acronyms—such as "FERC" in the D.C. Circuit, particularly in an appeal involving that agency—makes good sense. Using "the Commission," or "the Act" in the case of a statute, may be a suitable alternative if the acronym does not permit easy pronunciation. But writing the full name, "Federal Energy Regulatory Commission," each time would deliver quite a mouthful and might even slow down readers or induce skimming.[23]

On the other hand, as the D.C. Circuit Handbook states, an acronym created by the writer or otherwise unknown to most of the likely audience can confuse, with or without a glossary or initial full identification. If cavalier use of acronyms can leave judges adrift, consider the effect on other readers, who may also know much less about a case's underlying facts and law than the writer does.

Because it takes only a few words to avoid an acronym in favor of full identification, adapting the advice that closed Chapter 11's discussion of jargon appears sound here. If the writer senses that an acronym may leave judges or other audience members in the dark, the acronym probably will. When in doubt, spell it out.

---

[1]   *Acronym*, Merriam-Webster, http://www.merriam-webster.com/dictionary/acronym (visited Aug. 14, 2020).

[2]   680 F.3d 819 (D.C. Cir. 2012).

[3]   42 U.S.C. §§ 10101–10270 (2012).

[4]   Final Brief of Consolidated Petitioners at 48, Nat'l Ass'n of Regulatory Util. Comm'rs v. U.S. Dep't of Energy, 680 F.3d 819 (D.C. Cir. 2012) (Nos. 11–1066 & 11–1068).

[5]   Final Brief for Respondent at 24–25, Nat'l Ass'n of Regulatory Util. Comm'rs v. U.S. Dep't of Energy, 680 F.3d 819 (D.C. Cir. 2012) (Nos. 11–1066 & 11–1068).

[6]   *Nat'l Ass'n of Regulatory Util. Comm'rs*, *supra* note 2, 680 F.3d at 820 n.1.

[7]   *D.C. Circuit Handbook of Practice and Internal Procedures* 43 (2019); *see* Nat'l Ass'n of Regulatory Util. Comm'rs, *supra* note 2, 680 F.3d at 820 n.1.

[8]   753 F.3d 1304 (D.C. Cir. 2014).

[9]   *Id.* at 1320.

[10]   *Id.* at 1321.

[11]   Hilborn v. Metro Group Prop. & Cas. Ins. Co., No.2:12-cv-00636-BLW, 2014 WL 2506303, at *2 n.1 (D. Idaho June 3, 2014); Gomez v. State, 168 P.3d 1139, 1141 n.1 (Okla. Ct. Crim. App. 2007).

[12]   United States v. Rivera-Ortiz, No. 3:13-cr-00071-4, 2014 WL 6085387, at *4 n.1 (D. Conn. Nov. 13, 2014).

[13]   Dickerson v. Peake, No. 5:08-cv-122, 2011 WL 1258138, at *5 n.6 (M.D. Ga. Mar. 31, 2011).

[14]   Cotner v. Yoxheimer, No. 1:07-cv-1566, 2008 WL 2680872, at *2 n.1 (M.D. Pa. July 2, 2008).

[15]   Delaware Riverkeeper Network v. F.E.R.C., 753 F.3d 1304, 1321 (D.C. Cir. 2014).

[16]   *Id.*

[17]   No. 20-5106, 2020 WL 2515998 (D.C. Cir. May 15, 2020).

[18]   *Id.* *1. *See also* Allegheny Defense Project v. Federal Energy Regulatory Comm'n, 943 F.3d 496, 497 (D.C. Cir. 2019) (same).

[19]   *United States Court of Appeals, District of Columbia Circuit: About the Judges*, http://www.cadc.uscourts.gov/internet/home.nsf/content/judges (visited Jan. 25, 2016).

[20]   Watts v. Missouri-Kan-Tex. R.R. Co., 383 F.2d 571, 583 (5th Cir. 1967).

[21]   Waddy v. Globus Medical, Inc., No. 407CV075, 2008 WL 3861994, at *2 n.4 (S.D. Ga. Aug. 18, 2008).

[22]   Shoshone-Bannock Tribes of Fort Hall Reservation v. Shalala, 988 F. Supp. 1306, 1318 (D. Or. 1997), *reconsidered,* 999 F. Supp. 1395 (D. Or. 1998).

[23]   *See, e.g.*, Pierce v. North Dallas Honey Co., No. 3:19-CV-00410-X, 2020 WL 1047903, at *1 n.5 (N.D. Tex. Mar. 3, 2020) ("The court disfavors acronyms because they can render some sentences entirely unreadable. But given that the court was unable to pronounce '5-hydroxymethylfurfural' three times quickly, it will sadly proceed to use an acronym here for readability.").

CHAPTER 13

FOOTNOTES

■ ■ ■

Legal writing frequently means footnotes (which appear at the bottom of pages throughout the document), or endnotes (which appear together beginning after the final paragraph). This chapter generally uses the term "footnotes" to describe both devices because differences between their benefits and costs are few, and because electronic dissemination of legal publications often converts footnotes to endnotes.

Footnotes come in two basic varieties. "Citation footnotes" provide authorities and other sources for propositions advanced in the main text; "textual footnotes" contain sentences or paragraphs that pursue the main text's factual or legal discussion, or that introduce new thoughts, often with one or more citations. This chapter concerns the roles of footnotes in briefs and other court submissions, judicial opinions, and law review and bar journal articles.

"FLAUNTED PHI BETA KAPPA KEYS"

Footnotes in legal writing resemble marginally talented prize fighters who absorb repeated punishment, yet rise from the canvas each time for more. In 1936, Yale law professor Fred Rodell disparaged footnotes as "phony excrescences," and as "flaunted Phi Beta Kappa keys of legal writing" that test readers' patience.[1] Later critics have attacked footnotes as an "addiction . . . which mangles all legal writing,"[2] a "virus,"[3] "an insidious plague,"[4] and "a fierce distraction."[5] And as "a lazy form of writing,"[6] a "means of concealment,"[7] "hedges against forthright statements in the text,"[8] and "a safe refuge for untenable hypotheses."[9]

In the face of such relentless derision and evident contempt, what accounts for legal writers' continued reliance on footnotes? Much of the reason doubtlessly lies in the dominant legal writing culture, which too often conditions law students to begin equating "footnote proliferation" with wisdom even before they graduate. But footnoting also endures because most critics acknowledge important roles for efficient citation footnotes, which can enrich the writer's dialog with the reader. Most critics reserve the brunt of their scorn for (1) textual footnotes, and (2) citation footnotes that morph into "string citations" that provide a slew of authorities for propositions that need much less support or none at all.

CITATION FOOTNOTES

By identifying authorities for the writer's propositions, efficient citation footnotes enable readers to verify or respond. Economist John Kenneth Galbraith explained that "everyone, professional and lay reader alike, needs to know on occasion the credentials of a fact."[10] Citation footnotes, he added, also "provide an exceedingly good index of the care with which a subject has been researched."[11] But with a wary eye toward citation footnotes that serve the writer more than the reader, Professor Galbraith distinguished between what he called "adequacy and pedantry."[12]

Citations are essential to legal writing whose argumentation (to borrow Galbraith's explanation) "depends as much on authority as on logic."[13] Advocacy seeks to persuade readers, or to develop the law, by testing precedents and other doctrine, sometimes to their outer limits. Citations enable writers to share the fruits of the research and thought that produced the main text. Writers may also credit sources and authorities, an ethical obligation even when silence might not expose the writer to charges of plagiarism or copyright violation.[14] Because readers may be less familiar with the subject matter than the writer is, appending an explanatory parenthetical to a cited source can help unless the source's meaning is clear from the accompanying textual sentence or paragraph.

Efficiency, however, means handling string citations carefully. String cites may be useful, for example, to show an emerging or existing national trend or consensus,[15] but otherwise they may encumber the writing with distracting heft. The writer sometimes can avoid unwieldy strings by citing one or more recent binding or persuasive decisions that review precedents, and by ending the citation with a parenthetical: "(citing decisions)."

Most lawyers and courts continue placing citations in the main text of briefs and opinions, immediately following the sentence or passage to which they relate. But some commentators have argued lately for placing citations in footnotes instead.

"When citations are included within the main text, it is easier for the reader to see that authority supports the argument," say the traditionalists. "An argument with footnoted authorities . . . does not flow smoothly—the reader is forced to interrupt the reading of the main text to consult the notes."[16] Traditionalists also conclude that because footnotes appear below the main text, placing citations in a footnote can diminish their force.[17]

Legal writing professor Bryan A. Garner, however, argues that placing citations in footnotes enhances readability by clearing underbrush from the main text. Citations embedded in the main text, he says, are throwbacks to pre-word-processing days, when aligning footnotes in briefs and judicial opinions vexed the scrivener or typist. Garner's remedy today? "[P]ut citations—and generally only citations—in footnotes. And write in such a way that no reader would ever have to look at your footnotes to know what important authorities you're relying on. If you're quoting an opinion, you should—in the text—name the court you're quoting, the year in which it wrote, and (if necessary) the name of the case."[18]

TEXTUAL FOOTNOTES

U.S. Circuit Judge Abner J. Mikva assailed textual footnotes as "abominations" contrary to human physiology: "If God had intended the use of footnotes to be a norm, He would have put our eyes in vertically instead of horizontally."[19]

If a passage is important enough to include in the main text, the writer usually should place it there; if not, the writer usually should omit the passage altogether rather than consign it to a textual footnote. This approach usually means favoring a default position presented elsewhere in this book and explored in the rest of this chapter—when in doubt, leave it out.

Technology has made the default position more important than ever, but also easier to ignore than ever. The default position is "more important than ever" because so much published legal writing today appears immediately or eventually online, with footnotes converted to endnotes. Textual endnotes become even more inconvenient, unless the reader prints out the entire document or uses hyperlinking repeatedly to navigate through the entire document. "Reading endnotes," observed U.S. Circuit Judge Edward R. Becker, "involves fingers, mouth and neck—fingers for turning pages, mouth for licking fingers, and neck for head-twisting—an effort much more cumbersome than the head-bobbing that footnotes require."[20]

The default position is "easier to ignore than ever" because electronic searches and word processing can encourage footnote inflation. Lawyers can splurge by simply pressing a few keys, and the computer automatically renumbers the existing footnotes and realigns everything on the page. The outcome is neat and clean—and frequently annoying to readers.

FOOTNOTES IN BRIEFS AND OTHER COURT SUBMISSIONS

The door to advocates' textual footnotes remains slightly ajar. Judge Hugh R. Jones of the New York Court of Appeals was right that these footnotes are "largely to be deplored in brief writing and should be used sparingly and only when really appropriate."[21] When a court rule does not prohibit or discourage footnotes, they serve useful purposes only when they would help persuade the court. Efficient citation footnotes may identify sources and authorities, but textual footnotes tend to disrupt the argument.

Limited Usefulness

Veteran Supreme Court advocate Robert L. Stern advised that "[j]udges are much more likely to see and read what you write if it appears in the text; they will not be persuaded by what they do not read."[22] Frederick Bernays Wiener urged advocates to presume that footnoting in briefs "makes the writer's thoughts more difficult to follow—and hence far less likely to persuade the judicial reader."[23]

Wiener found a purpose for advocates' textual footnotes that "indicate qualifications to statements in the text, where such qualifications would interrupt the thought if they remained in the text"; or for footnotes that "include citations on points of secondary importance."[24] But he cautioned against footnoted responses to an adversary's point: "[U]nless the opposition argument is utterly devoid of support in the record, it deserves reply in the text of your brief, and it is only your case that will be hurt when you drop your own views down to a footnote."[25]

A textual footnote may also treat a complex point that the advocate does not wish to press, but also does not wish to abandon because the court might consider it during oral argument, on supplemental briefing, or later on appeal. Preserving the point may seem wise, but some courts reportedly disregard arguments raised exclusively in footnotes.[26]

Judge Jones added that "if the text invites collateral questions or speculation, a short footnote may avert curiosity and thus diversion."[27] But U.S. Circuit Judge Ruggero J. Aldisert warned advocates that "marginal comments, often with piddling objections to minor points in the opponent's brief or the lower court's opinion, add little to and subtract much" from the advocacy's force.[28] Textual footnotes delving into collateral matters might display the advocate's knowledge or research, but Judge Aldisert urged professional modesty: "Judges do not need a show-and-tell exercise to reveal how smart you are."[29]

Abuse

A final cautionary note deserves mention. Trial courts and appellate courts alike remain alert for advocates' efforts to use excessive footnotes, single-spaced or in a smaller font, to circumvent maximum-page limits established by court rules for briefs and other submissions. Judges read submissions for a living, and they are unlikely to be fooled by the ruse. And judges have long memories for lawyers with track records that are short on integrity or candor.

Counsel's attempted circumvention may lead the court to strike the brief or other submission, obliging the advocate to refile and face the prospect of an alienated court.[30] The court's early sanction may tarnish the client's impressions of counsel, and may even lead a disgruntled client to consider afterwards whether arousing judicial animosity might have contributed to an adverse outcome. Attempted circumvention also invites skepticism about whether counsel who would cut corners on a court rule would also cut corners on research and factual or legal argument.

The ABA Model Rules of Professional Conduct specify that "[a]s advocate, a lawyer zealously asserts the client's position under the rules of the adversary system."[31] The specification leaves no room for seeking to tilt the playing field in a client's favor by evading court rules about page limits. Counsel's sharp practice can exact a heavy price because the U.S. Court of Appeals for the Seventh Circuit is right that a reputation for integrity is a lawyer's "bread and butter."[32] The risk of forfeiting this nourishment is not worth errant footnotes in a brief or other court submission. A track record of adhering to the rules remains a much healthier diet.

JUDICIAL FOOTNOTES

Three months into my clerkship with Judge Jones, the judge felt I was ready to cut my teeth on drafting part of an opinion. Barely out of law school, I looked forward to seeing my words between a reporter's hard covers for the first time. As I prepared the draft, I did what came naturally to a green law clerk. I wrote some textual footnotes. A few days later, Judge Jones returned my draft, minus nearly all of them.

Judge Jones delivered a valuable lesson about why judges should avoid textual footnotes, except ones that genuinely advance decision making or otherwise serve a useful purpose. Judicial footnotes can leave readers annoyed by the usual distractions, but that is not all.

Judges write opinions not as private citizens, but as public officers vested with constitutional authority to publish decisions with the force of law. Judicial footnotes compel lawyers to spend their time (and the client's money) weighing the footnotes' possible precedential effect in later cases, when judges or parties may cite or distinguish text or citations that appear anywhere in a prior opinion. In our system grounded in precedent and concern about access to the courts, judicial footnoting without principled self-restraint can impose a high price on the administration of justice.

Judicial footnotes may leave later lawyers and courts in the dark because courts themselves have achieved no consensus concerning the precedential force of their footnotes. The darkness may affect future application of both binding and persuasive precedents. A footnote may suggest that the court did not deem its content sufficiently important to warrant inclusion in the main text, but a footnote may also suggest that the court did not deem the content so unimportant to warrant exclusion.[33]

A judicial footnote can also work mischief by advancing a proposition that is supported by little or no authority, and that may even border on being incorrect as a matter of law.[34] But unsupported dictum in today's footnote can become tomorrow's holding when one or more courts cite it, sometimes without further analysis or support.

Judicial Trends

Judicial footnoting conventions show some halting signs of change in recent years. In the mid-1980s, Professor Milton Handler criticized the Supreme Court's "addiction to . . . voluminous footnotes which seem to increase term after term."[35] Majority, concurring, and dissenting opinions carried 3460 footnotes in the 1984 Term alone, leading Professor Handler to complain that "it is not the function of the highest court of the land to produce a new edition of Corpus Juris in its opinions."[36]

In 2012, Judge Aldisert called the Supreme Court still "an institution that gorges on the unnecessary and spits out footnotes in a sort of postgraduate show-and-tell."[37] Some Justices, however, have resisted footnotes in recent years.[38] Justice Stephen G. Breyer, for example, says that "either a point is sufficiently significant to make, in which case it should be in the text, or it is not, in which case, don't make it."[39] In conversations with her law clerks, Justice Sandra Day O'Connor expressed an attitude that disparaged footnotes: "If you have something to say, just say it. Don't weasel around down in the brush."[40]

Some lower court judges have also inched away from footnotes. Judge Mikva said that using footnotes often "perverts judicial opinions."[41] Judge Posner advocates opinions with "no footnotes."[42] U.S. District Judge Robert E. Keeton said that "drafting an opinion with no . . . footnotes is harder work," but that "the result, if well done, is a clearer and more readable opinion, with fewer ambiguities."[43]

Usefulness

Judge Aldisert found limited useful purposes for judicial footnotes, such as (1) to "dispose of collateral issues, controlled by precedent, that would disrupt flow or organization of text," (2) to "record related issues not reached," (3) to "set forth trial testimony that supports facts in text," or (4) to "respond to concurring or dissenting opinions."[44]

"[I]f the body of the text reads persuasively in its own,"[45] Judge Becker wrote, "judicious use of footnotes allows judges to communicate most effectively with their diverse audiences"[46] while omitting "material that is peripheral to the essential meaning of the case."[47] The primary audience, the parties and their lawyers, can benefit from footnotes (1) demonstrating that the court considered collateral claims not discussed in the text, (2) "elaborating the reasoning stated succinctly in the body of the opinion," or

(3) "furnishing a fuller understanding of the background and nuances of the case."[48]

Judge Becker also approved of (1) footnotes containing citations, statutory quotations, historical matter or theoretical discourse that reduces the need to "guess about the building blocks of the court's reasoning," (2) footnotes that "buttress the holding, qualify it, or otherwise reflect on its utility,"[49] and (3) footnotes that question the state of the law, recommend law reform to the legislature, or respond to concurrences or dissents.[50]

Judge Becker's last prong leaves room for judicial footnotes whose dictum invites development of legal doctrine. Chapter 3 references a prominent example, Justice Harlan Fiske Stone's celebrated Footnote 4 in *United States v. Carolene Products Co.* (1938), which resulted in transformation of constitutional analysis.[51]

The judges' debate invites a George Orwell-style Rule of Reason similar to that explored in Chapter 6, but grounded in rhetorical judicial restraint. "No footnotes . . . ," then-Judge Breyer promised when President Clinton nominated him to the Supreme Court in 1994. But then the nominee hedged: "or as few as possible."[52]

LAW REVIEW AND BAR JOURNAL FOOTNOTES

Chapter 16 will encourage practicing lawyers, consistent with their other personal and professional obligations, to consider writing or co-writing articles in law reviews or bar association journals. Reviews and journals seek to enrich the legal dialog, and efficient citation footnotes identify sources and authorities necessary to sustain argument and commentary.

Law review articles are also known for their dense textual footnotes, which seek to entice readers into a game of vertical "visual tennis," with their eyes continually bobbing from the top of the page to the bottom.[53] Textual bar journal notes (which usually appear as endnotes in both print and electronic versions) tend to be sparser but can produce similar distractions. When readers grow frustrated, law review and bar journal textual notes may go unread. So might much of the main text if readers turn away altogether before the end.

The apparent all-time winner of the "most footnotes in a law review article" sweepstakes is Arnold S. Jacobs, a securities lawyer whose 1987 *New York Law School Law Review* article came with 4824 footnotes.[54] One law school librarian anointed Jacobs "the Hank Aaron of footnotes,"[55] though Jacobs' record—footnotes on steroids—has outlasted Aaron's.

Jacobs also had much more behind-the-scenes help than the Braves slugger, who homered 755 times without help from the dugout. Dozens of

Jacobs' footnotes were variants of "*See infra* [or *See supra*] text accompanying note ___," guideposts routinely added by student editors who assume that law review readers, unlike readers of other literature for ages, need distracting footnoted assistance to shepherd them through a text that good writing itself can make comprehensible. Or routinely added by student editors who assume that nearly every sentence in the main text needs footnoted support or explanation.

Some academic law review articles feature pages that contain as much as one-third text and two-thirds footnotes. Footnotes sometimes consume an entire page, without a single line of text at the top. "[O]ne always suspects," said Judge Aldisert, that "a law review article whose footnotes continually creep up over half of the page has been poorly written—it could have been rewritten to get rid of at least some of those footnotes if the author cared enough or had enough time."[56]

Chapter 2 cautioned that "just because a writer puts something down on paper does not necessarily mean that people will read it, wholly or even in large part." Writers must Earn the Right to a Reader. Sure ways to forfeit this right in law review or bar journal articles are to use textual footnotes as depositories or waste baskets for material that would be better excised, or to cite authority for every proposition, including propositions that reasonable readers understand need no citation. Writers emotionally unwilling to prune extraneous textual material may feel tempted simply to "drop it into a footnote," though pressing the "delete" key would encourage readers to focus more closely on the central arguments.

"There is but one art—to omit!," said Scottish writer Robert Louis Stevenson, who lamented that, "O if I only knew how to omit, I would ask no other knowledge."[57] Self-discipline to omit textual footnotes is particularly crucial for law review and bar journal writers. Readers tired of footnoted distractions can heed the advice of Stanford legal historian Lawrence M. Friedman, who urges "putting down that law review and picking up a good novel. It does wonders for the soul."[58]

"ANYTHING WORTH SAYING. . . ."

In the preface to his lengthy 1963 classic book, *The Language of the Law*, Professor David Mellinkoff reassured readers. "The footnotes are for reference only," he wrote. "Anything worth saying has been said in the body of the text."[59] This warranty got the book off on the right foot.

More than 250 years ago, Enlightenment philosopher Jean-Jacques Rousseau candidly appraised the endnotes in his book, *Discourse on the Origin and Foundations of Inequality Among Men*. "I have added some notes to this work, following my lazy custom of working in fits and starts," he wrote. "These notes sometimes stray so far from the subject that they are not good to read with the text. I have therefore relegated them to the end. . . . Those who have the courage to begin again will be able to amuse themselves the second time in beating the bushes, and try to go through the notes. There will be little harm if others do not read them at all."[60]

---

[1]   Fred Rodell, *Goodbye to Law Reviews*, 23 Va. L. Rev. 38, 40 (1936); *see also* Fred Rodell, *Goodbye to Law Reviews—Revisited*, 48 Va. L. Rev. 279, 281 (1962).

[2]   W. Duane Benton, *Developments In the Law—Legal Citation*, 86 Yale L.J. 197, 199 (1976) (reviewing A Uniform System of Citation (12th ed. 1976)).

[3]   Kenneth Lasson, *Scholarship Amok: Excesses in the Pursuit of Truth and Tenure*, 103 Harv. L. Rev. 926, 939 (1990).

[4]   Arthur D. Austin, *Footnotes as Product Differentiation*, 40 Vand. L. Rev. 1131, 1133 (1987).

[5]   Tom Goldstein & Jethro K. Lieberman, The Lawyer's Guide to Writing Well 108 (2d ed. 2002); *see also, e.g.*, Bryan A. Garner, The Elements of Legal Style 93 (2d ed. 2002) (calling footnotes "the netherworld"); Hugh R. Jones, *Appellate Advocacy, Written and Oral*, 47 J. Mo. Bar 297, 300 (June 1991) (calling footnotes "the darlings of some pedants"); Abner J. Mikva, *Goodbye to Footnotes*, 56 U. Colo. L. Rev. 647, 647 (1985) (the use of footnotes "has spread like a fungus").

[6]   Richard A. Posner, The Federal Courts: Challenge and Reform 352 (1996).

[7]   David Mellinkoff, Legal Writing: Sense and Nonsense 94 (1982).

[8]   *Id.*

[9]   G.W. Bowersock, *The Art of the Footnote*, 53 Am. Scholar 54, 61 (Winter 1983/84).

[10]   John Kenneth Galbraith, The Great Crash 1929, at xxiv (3d ed. 1972).

[11]   *Id.*

[12]   *Id.*

[13]   Helen A. Anderson, *Are Citations on the Way Down? The Case Against Footnotes*, Wash. St. B. News 28–30 (Dec. 2001).

[14]   *E.g.*, Elizabeth Fajans & Mary R. Falk, Scholarly Writing for Law Students, ch. 6 (2005); Eugene Volokh, Academic Legal Writing 334–38 (4th ed. 2010).

[15]   *E.g.*, K.K. DuVivier, *String Citations—Part II*, 29 Colo. Law. 67 (Sept. 2000).

[16]   Helen A. Anderson, *supra* note 13 at 28.

[17]   *E.g.*, George Rose Smith, *A Primer of Opinion Writing, For Four New Judges*, 21 Ark. L. Rev. 197, 211 (1967).

[18]   Bryan A. Garner, Legal Writing In Plain English 95 (2d ed. 2013). *See also, e.g.*, Bryan A. Garner, *The Citational Footnote*, 7 Scribes J. Legal Writing 97 (2000); John Minor Wisdom, *"How I Write" Essays*, 4 Scribes J. Legal Writing 83, 86 (1993) ("Citations belong in a footnote: even one full citation . . . breaks the thought; two, three, or more in one massive paragraph are an abomination.").

[19]   Abner J. Mikva, *Law Reviews, Judicial Opinions, and Their Relationship to Writing*, 30 Stetson L. Rev. 521, 524 (2000).

[20]   Edward R. Becker, *In Praise of Footnotes*, 74 Wash. U. L. Q. 1, 12 (1996).

[21]   Hugh R. Jones, *supra* note 5 at 300; *see also* Nancy L. Schultz & Louis J. Sirico, Jr., Legal Writing and Other Lawyering Skills § 27.01[e][iv], at 312 (3d ed. 1998).

[22]   Robert L. Stern, Appellate Practice in the United States 325 (1981).

[23]   Frederick Bernays Wiener, Effective Appellate Advocacy 145 (Christopher T. Lutz & William Pannill eds., rev. ed. 2004).

[24]   *Id.* at 145–46.

[25]   *Id.* at 146.

[26]   Bryan A. Garner, The Redbook: A Manual on Legal Style 139 (2d ed. 2006).

[27]   Hugh R. Jones, *supra* note 5 at 300.

[28]   Ross Guberman, Point Made: How to Write Like the Nation's Top Advocates 147 (2011) (quoting Judge Aldisert).

[29]   *Id.*

[30]   *E.g.*, Debra Cassens Weiss, *DOJ Is Latest Litigant to Face Judge's Ire For Lengthy Footnotes*, A.B.A. J. (posted Aug. 17, 2020) (ordering U.S. Department of Justice to refile reply

brief that failed to comply with local federal district court rule that prohibits "excessive" footnotes); Conference of State Bank Supervisors v. Office of the Comptroller of the Currency, No. 1:17-cv-00763 (U.S.D.C. D.D.C) (Order of July 28, 2017) (party's "excessive footnoting both violates [the applicable court rule] and appears to be an effort to circumvent page limitations"), discussed in Debra Cassens Weiss, *Federal Judge Cites "Excessive Footnoting" and Imposes Page Limit For Revised Government Brief*, A.B.A. J. (posted July 31, 2017); Free Range Content, Inc. v. Google Inc., No. 14-cv-02329, 2015 WL 5029480 (N.D. Calif. Nov. 16, 2015) (striking plaintiff's motion papers, which exceeded page limits by using 451 lines of single-spaced footnotes, the equivalent of more than 16 double-spaced pages; ordering plaintiff's counsel to file papers that did not exceed 25 pages, with "no footnotes"); Brantley v. Ferrell Elec., Inc., 112 F. Supp.3d 1348, 2015 WL 3541552 *27 n.17 (S.D. Ga. 2015) (cautioning plaintiff's counsel against further use of excessive single-spaced footnotes to evade maximum page limits for filed motions).

[31]   ABA Model Rules of Professional Conduct, Preamble [2] (2019).

[32]   Harlyn Sales Corp. Profit Sharing Plan v. Kemper Fin. Servs., 9 F.3d 1263, 1269 (7th Cir. 1993).

[33]   *See, e.g.*, Abner J. Mikva, *Goodbye to Footnotes*, 56 U. Colo. L. Rev. 647, 649 (1985).

[34]   *Cf.* Richard A. Posner, The Federal Courts: Challenge and Reform 352, 353 (1996).

[35]   Milton Handler, *The Supreme Court's Footnote Addiction*, 58 N.Y. St. B.J. 18, 18 (Dec. 1986).

[36]   *Id.* at 20.

[37]   Ruggero J. Aldisert, *Opinion Writers and Opinion Readers*, 31 Cardozo L. Rev. 1, 41 (2009).

[38]   James J. Kilpatrick, *Slow Days Lately At the Land's Highest Court*, Augusta (Ga.) Chronicle, Mar. 5, 2006, at A5 (discussing Chief Justice Roberts and Justices Kennedy and Souter); Robert E. Keeton, *"How I Write" Essays*, 4 Scribes J. Legal Writing 31, 34 (1993) (discussing Justices O'Connor and Kennedy).

[39]   *Id. See also* Stephen Breyer, *So They Say: Opinion on Footnotes*, 81 A.B.A. J. 39 (Oct. 1995).

[40]   Kent D. Syverud, *Lessons From Working For Sandra Day O'Connor*, 58 Stan. L. Rev. 1731, 1731 (2006).

[41]   Abner J. Mikva, *supra* note 5 at 648.

[42]   Richard A. Posner, Divergent Paths 270 (2016).

[43]   Robert E. Keeton, *"How I Write" Essays, supra* note 36 at 35.

[44]   Ruggero J. Aldisert, Opinion Writing 212 (2d ed. 2009).

[45]   Edward R. Becker, *supra* note 20 at 8.

[46]   *Id.* at 1.

[47]   *Id.* at 13.

[48]   *Id.* at 5. *See also, e.g., Judge Pierre N. Leval, Interview Conducted by Bryan A. Garner*, 15 Scribes J. Legal Writing 49 (2013) ("If it would be helpful to explain something a little further, but if it distracts from the central argument, it's often helpful to put it in a footnote.").

[49]   Edward R. Becker, *supra* note 20 at 5.

[50]   *Id.* at 6–7.

[51]   304 U.S. 144, 152 n.4 (1938).

[52]   Ruth Marcus, *Judge Breyer Gets Day in Rose Garden*, Wash. Post (May 17, 1994).

[53]   William R. Slomanson, *The Bottom Line: Footnote Logic in Law Review Writing*, 7 Legal Reference Servs. Q. 47, 54 (1987) (calling the game "an enjoinable nuisance").

[54]   Arnold S. Jacobs, *An Analysis of Section 16 of the Securities Exchange Act of 1934*, 32 N.Y. L. Sch. L. Rev. 209 (1987).

[55]   Kris Oser, *Numerous Notes No Shot In Foot*, Nat'l L.J., Jan. 16, 1989, at 35 (quoting Yale librarian Fred Shapiro).

[56]   J.M. Balkin, *The Footnote*, 83 Nw. U. L. Rev. 275, 277 (1989) (quoting Judge Aldisert).

[57]   Robert Louis Stevenson, *To Thomas Stevenson, in* 1 The Letters of Robert Louis Stevenson to His Family and Friends 339 (Sidney Colvin ed., 1899).

[58]   Lawrence M. Friedman, *"How I Write" Essays*, 4 Scribes J. Legal Writing 3, 5–6 (1993).

[59]   David Mellinkoff, The Language of the Law viii (1963).

[60]   Roger D. Masters, The Political Philosophy of Rousseau 108–09 (1968).

PART 6

VERSATILITY

■ ■ ■

Practicing lawyers commonly write as their clients' representatives, but Part Six selects leading opportunities open to lawyers who also wish to write in non-representational roles. Chapter 14 discusses legislative drafting, stressing plain English. Some lawyers draft as a legislator's staff member or in the legislature's central research office. Other lawyers draft in compensated or uncompensated service to legislatures, advocacy groups, or other organizations.

Chapters 15 and 16 treat what commentators sometimes call "extracurricular writing," lawyers' publications about legal topics unrelated to specific matters on their calendar, and sometimes even about topics unrelated to law.[1] If a lawyer's personal and professional circumstances permit (an important consideration, as these two chapters discuss), the lawyer's public voice can reach wider audiences than the small circle of clients, opponents, and judges who ordinarily read representational writing.

Chapter 15 explores extracurricular writing in newspaper op-ed columns and letters-to-the-editor. Chapter 16 explores extracurricular writing or co-writing in law reviews, state and local bar journals, and blogs.

---

[1]   *E.g.*, Joel Cohen, *An Interview with Judge Richard A. Posner: Do One's 'Real World' Activities—Writing, Theorizing, Blogging—Negatively Impact One's Judging?*, 100 A.B.A. J. 52 (2014); Adam Liptak, *California Prosecutor's Novel Gets Her Bumped From a Case*, N.Y. Times, Oct. 9, 2006, at 10.

CHAPTER 14

DRAFTING LEGISLATION IN PLAIN ENGLISH

∎ ∎ ∎

In 1982, Professor Guido Calabresi chronicled the "statutorification" of American law.[1] Within a few decades, he explained, the nation had moved "from a legal system dominated by the common law, divined by courts, to one in which statutes, enacted by legislatures, have become the primary source of law."[2]

The move presents distinct challenges to the administration of justice. In 1947, with "statutorification" still in its relative infancy, one commentator reported that "[n]early everyone complains about the obscurity of statutes."[3] In the 1960s, as the plain English movement began influencing legislative expression, legal drafting scholar Reed Dickerson reported that much federal, state, and local legislation remained infected by "confusions, turgidities, circumlocutions, and expressions of downright gobbledygook."[4] In the 21st century, Judge Mark Painter of the Ohio Court of Appeals concurs that "[f]or sheer unfathomability, statutes are probably the champions."[5]

In our nation based on consent of the governed, sheer unfathomability undermines the rule of law. We live (as Calabresi put it) in the "Age of Statutes," when federal, state, and local legislation directly or indirectly affects the lives of nearly all Americans.[6] This profound effect confers responsibilities on the men and women who draft laws and administrative regulations. Dean Roger C. Cramton is right that "[s]impler statutes and regulations written in 'plain English' might be more readily followed without resort to professional advice."[7]

From the earliest stages until final enactment, legislative drafters should strive for the greatest possible measure of plain English expression whenever they can reasonably foresee that the persons directly or indirectly affected by a contemplated measure would include segments of the public who hold no legal training or law degree. The Missouri legislature's Joint Committee on Legislative Research recites the standard, which closely tracks the fundamentals of effective legal writing stressed throughout this book: "The essentials of good bill drafting are accuracy, brevity, clarity, and simplicity."[8]

"BABY TALK"?

A quick visit to a physical or online law library confirms the contemporary dominance of legislation and its accompanying administrative regulations. An annual compilation of the United States Statutes at Large, and any similar annual state legislative compilation, now dwarf their slim counterparts for almost any 19th century year. The United States Code and state codes, which are subject-by-subject statutory compilations, consume entire shelves. So do the Code of Federal Regulations (subject-by-subject compilations of federal administrative law) and state administrative counterparts. Adding to this array are codes, charters, ordinances, and rules enacted by city councils, boards of supervisors, and similar local legislative bodies.

Critics sometimes scoff at calls to demystify these sources of law with plain English drafting. The gist of the critique is that statutes and administrative law speak not to lay readers, but to lawyers and judges whose legal training equips them to grasp legal nuance and technicality.[9] "The language of our legislation," says one critic, "cannot be reduced to baby talk for consumption by the masses."[10]

Intricate legal doctrine does sometimes resist expression in plain English, but critics who routinely denigrate plain English drafting overlook a core purpose of statutes and regulations in our national life. By making laws more comprehensible, plain English can help law-abiding people play by the rules, without having to endure a frustrating, frequently avoidable, and ultimately self-defeating game of "hide the ball" mired in legalese. "The language of the law," said U.S. Circuit Judge Learned Hand decades ago, "must not be foreign to the ears of those who are to obey it."[11]

THE DRAFTER'S AUDIENCE OF NON-LAWYERS

Knowing the Audience, the compass discussed in Chapter 2, provides a useful start for plain English drafting. The audience for legislative and administrative drafters can include both lawyers and non-lawyers, and the second group often outnumbers the first.

The legislative drafter's non-lawyer audience begins with the lawmakers themselves, many or most of whom in a typical Congress or state or local legislature hold no law degree. Legislators may vote based on their understanding gleaned from reading the bill, from following floor debate, or from reading bill summaries written by staff members, some of whom may be lawyers. But reliance on secondary sources invites risk when the bill, and not the debating points or the summaries, becomes law.

Following enactment, a statute's application and enforcement may depend on decision making by public officials who have no formal legal training or sustained access to a legal staff. Business people and other non-lawyer professionals also frequently consult statutes that regulate their affairs.

The drafter's non-lawyer audience also may extend to people from all walks of life whom the enactment may affect, a class that may number in the thousands or more. Congress and state legislatures recognize this potential breadth by posting filed bills and statutory codes on official websites for the general public's inspection and downloading.[12] Local legislative bodies also typically post their bills, enactments, and regulations.

In some fields of law that touch on everyday life, many people cannot afford to retain a lawyer, or else may feel more comfortable with self-representation (proceeding *pro se*). Lawyers are expensive, and self-representation remains a right in most circumstances.

For example, at least one party proceeds without a lawyer in more than half of divorce and other family law cases, usually because the party finds representation too costly or intrusive.[13] The divorce act, and other domestic relations statutes that regulate family relationships, reflect standards sculpted by legislators and courts over time. These statutes should remain at least as accessible to the general public as summaries, official forms, and other publications written (usually in plain English) by government authorities, or by state or local bar associations. These sources should complement rather than supplant good faith efforts by legislatures and agencies to articulate the law as plainly as possible to lay audiences.

Plain English does more than enhance meaning when members of the public examine statute books and other published sources of public and private law, as the public has every right to do. Plain English also enhances the capacity of lay readers to provide their elected representatives commentary about pending bills, to comment on pending administrative action, and then to conform their conduct to the law or make more reasoned decisions about whether to consult a lawyer or other specialist. Most Americans may not seek out these opportunities much of the time, but their disinclination does not diminish the entitlement of Americans who do.

THE "LEGISLATIVE DRAFTER'S PRESUMPTION"

Legislative drafters should begin from the presumption that plain English would enable lay persons potentially affected by an enactment to grasp its essence and determine whether to seek legal counsel or other professional advice. The presumption favoring plain English remains rebuttable, but only for sound reasons because (as the Uniform Law Conference of Canada recommends) law "should be written as much as possible in ordinary language, using technical terminology only if precision requires it."[14] Similar to baseball's rule that a tie goes to the runner, the benefit of the doubt should go to plain English.

The Legislative Drafter's Presumption is a corollary of a presumption that typically confers personal responsibility on the general public.[15] In civil and criminal matters, people are conclusively presumed to know the law, and thus usually may not plead lack of knowledge when litigating against the government or a private party.[16] For this standard sometimes to resemble reality rather than merely to survive as a legal fiction that snares the unsuspecting, legislative drafters should strive when possible to offer lay people—that is, most people—fair opportunity to know the law that the legal system conclusively presumes that they know.

Knowledge of the law depends on access, and access means more than the mere opportunity to inspect bills, statutes, or regulations in a law library or on an official government website. Where drafters can reasonably foresee an audience rich in lay people, access also means making reasonable efforts to provide these non-lawyers, to the extent possible, a fair opportunity to figure out generally what the law expects from them.

COMPLEXITIES AND SIMPLICITIES

Professor Frank Grad explained why legal intricacies may rebut the Legislative Drafter's Presumption: "Many problems that need legislative resolution are complex and difficult. To pretend that they are susceptible of 'plain' statement is . . . misleading. . . . We need complex language to state complex problems of law or fact."[17]

Professor Grad's instruction remains sound because in some fields of law, understanding statutes and other official sources indeed depends on knowledge, background, and context beyond laypersons' ready grasp. Intricacies may have emerged as a bill drafted in plain English worked its way through the compromises and other give-and-take that often characterize the legislative process. The passage of time may also thwart plain English when today's bill amends enactments whose language and supportive judicial interpretations, written years ago, handcuff drafters who would opt for plainer expression if they were starting fresh. Statutes and other sources of law frequently vex even legally trained judges who must ascertain their meaning and apply them in accordance with their terms.

But legislative drafters should hesitate to sacrifice plain English when plainness remains an achievable goal. From Chapter 5, recall Sir Winston Churchill's observation that "out of intense complexities, intense simplicities emerge."[18] Law may not always prove as complex as it first appears, and disciplined drafters adept at plain English can often overcome barriers that legalese would impose. When plain English drafting remains within reach, its virtues today remain as central as they were in the 16th century, when British King Edward VI urged Parliament to make statutes "more plain and short, to the intent that men might better understand them."[19]

---

[1]   Guido Calabresi, A Common Law For the Age of Statutes 44 (1982).

[2]   *Id.* at 1.

[3]   Alfred F. Conard, *New Ways to Write Laws*, 56 Yale L.J. 458, 458 (1947).

[4]   Reed Dickerson, The Fundamentals of Legal Drafting § 1.1, at 2 (1986).

[5]   Mark Painter, The Legal Writer 16 (2d ed. 2003).

[6]   Guido Calabresi, *supra* note 1 at 1.

[7]   Roger C. Cramton, *Delivery of Legal Services to Ordinary Americans*, 44 Case W. Res. L. Rev. 531, 562 (1994).

[8]   Missouri Comm. on Legislative Research, *The Essentials of Bill Drafting in the Missouri General Assembly* 1 (2011).

[9]   Brian Hunt, *Plain Language In Legislative Drafting: An Achievable Objective Or a Laudable Ideal?*, 24 Statute L. Rev. 112, 114–16 (2003).

[10]   Brian Hunt, *Plain Language In Legislative Drafting: Is It Really the Answer?*, 23 Statute L. Rev. 24, 44 (2002).

[11]   Learned Hand, *Is There a Common Will?*, in The Spirit of Liberty 56 (I. Dilliard ed. 1953).

[12]   *See, e.g., Past Sessions Information, Mo. Senate*, http://www.senate.mo.gov/pastsessions. htm (visited Jan. 23, 2016); *Bill Information, Mo. House of Representatives*, http://www.house.mo. gov/sitemap.aspx?pid=13 (visited Jan. 23, 2016).

[13]   Douglas E. Abrams et al., Contemporary Family Law 994–95 (5th ed. 2019).

[14]   Douglas E. Abrams, *Plain-English Drafting for the Age of Statutes*, 88 Mich. B.J. 50, 51 (June 2009); Robert C. Dick, Legal Drafting in Plain Language 229 (3d ed. 1995) (quoting § 31 of the Legislative Drafting Conventions of the Drafting Section of the Uniform Law Conference of Canada).

[15]   Elonis v. United States, 575 U.S. 723, 135 S. Ct. 2001, 2009 (2015).

[16]   *E.g.*, Hicks v. State, 419 S.W.3d 555, 558 (Tex. Ct. App. 2013).

[17]   Frank P. Grad, *Legislative Drafting as Legal Problem Solving—Form Follows Function*, in Drafting Documents in Plain Language 481, 489 (Duncan A. MacDonald ed., 1979).

[18]   Manuel L. Real, *Symposium on Mass Torts: What Evil Have We Wrought: Class Action, Mass Torts, and Settlement*, 31 Loy. L.A. L. Rev. 437, 437 (1998) (quoting Churchill).

[19]   Office of the Scottish Parliamentary Counsel, *Plain Language and Legislation* 1 (2006) (quoting King Edward VI).

CHAPTER 15

WRITING NEWSPAPER OP-ED COLUMNS AND LETTERS-TO-THE-EDITOR

■ ■ ■

Most lawyers never write on the editorial pages of national, regional, or local newspapers. After 35 years as the prominent editor and publisher of *The Tennessean* and *USA TODAY*, John L. Seigenthaler said that he could "count on one hand" the number of letters-to-the-editor and unsolicited op-ed columns (essays appearing "opposite the editorial page") he had received from lawyers.[1]

Seigenthaler was speaking about lost opportunities because writing on newspaper editorial pages can enable lawyers to influence the public dialog as they enhance their own professional standing. The *New York Times* says that writers seek out the editorial pages "for the influence, for the chance to reach an audience, to say something that's been bothering them, driving them crazy, something that no one else seems to be saying."[2] Stimuli such as these can motivate lawyers as much as they motivate other thoughtful writers.

Lawyers can reach out to essentially lay audiences with letters-to-the-editor or op-eds about legal doctrine, recent legislation, or recent court decisions. Lawyers also can write about public policy matters that touch on law, such as school bond issues or foster care funding. Lawyers can even use the editorial pages to share thoughts about parenting, personal health, or other social or cultural questions that have little or nothing to do with law or public policy.

Contemporary technology has changed the face of journalism, but the nation's editorial pages have survived the rise of satellite and cable television, online news sources, blogs, social media, and other competitors for the public's attention. Writers from all walks of life still compete for space on these influential pages because lawmakers, policy makers, and others pay attention in a newspaper's print edition or on its website. Many leading newspapers receive 100 or more unsolicited op-ed submissions each day.[3] The *New York Times* receives roughly 1200 each week.[4]

The *St. Louis Post-Dispatch* receives hundreds of letters-to-the-editor weekly, with space to publish only about 60.[5] Some smaller papers publish many of the well-written letters they receive, but competition for space remains fiercer in larger papers.

THRESHOLD CONSIDERATIONS ABOUT EXTRACURRICULAR WRITING: RESPONSIBILITY, REWARDS, AND WISDOM

This chapter and the next one concern "extracurricular writing," a term that describes publications about topics that are unrelated to specific matters in the lawyer's practice, and sometimes even unrelated to law. Like anyone else, lawyers hold essentially free rein to write about health, sports, or similar social or cultural matters. But lawyers who contemplate writing about matters touching on law or public policy should first calibrate the three considerations discussed below in this section. Calibration should precede both ventures into this chapter's extracurricular forums (newspaper editorial pages), and ventures into Chapter 16's extracurricular forums (law reviews, bar association journals, and blogs).

The first two considerations—Responsibility and Rewards—normally point toward proceeding with desired extracurricular writing, but in some cases the third consideration—Wisdom—may not. Writing about law or public policy can help fulfill the lawyer's *responsibility* to join public discussion, and it can *reward* the lawyer by stimulating personal and professional enrichment before a potentially vast audience. But the contemplated writing may be *unwise*, for example because the lawyer's arguments or conclusions might antagonize current and prospective clients, or because the lawyer's public or private employer might discourage or even prohibit such writing.

This section discusses these three threshold considerations. Chapter 16 returns to the wisdom prong with a significant added wrinkle: Lawyers can compose letters-to-the-editor or op-eds relatively quickly, but extracurricular writing in one or more of Chapter 16's forums—law reviews, bar association journals, or blogs—require sustained time commitments that can intrude unduly on the lawyer's other personal and professional obligations to family and clients.

Responsibility

Extracurricular writing about law or public policy can help lawyers fulfill a responsibility, recited in the ABA Model Rules of Professional Conduct, to perform as "public citizens" who "further the public's understanding of and confidence in the rule of law and the justice system."[6] The recitation reflects lofty aspirations. Sir Francis Bacon called "every man a debtor to his profession."[7] President Theodore Roosevelt said that every person "owes some of his time to the upbuilding of the profession to which he belongs."[8] Extracurricular writing in newspapers, law reviews, bar journals, or blogs can help lawyers repay this debt with commentary that advances what Justice Louis D. Brandeis called the "processes of education."[9]

Rewards

Time spent on extracurricular writing normally brings little or no immediate remuneration to lawyers who are accustomed to billing for client representation. But extracurricular writing can bring the lawyer valuable short-term and long-term rewards—advertising, learning and education, and professional satisfaction.

Advertising. Publication suggests expertise, which can impress current and prospective clients, and can facilitate networking. Published writings (or links to them) may interest clients, friends, professional acquaintances, legislators and other policymakers, and bloggers. Links to these writings can enhance the lawyer's resume, the law firm's webpage or blog, or the web pages of the newspaper, law review, or bar journal that publishes the work. Published lawyers can also distribute reprints or links at bar association and other professional meetings. Westlaw, Lexis, and other electronic databases typically carry downloadable published articles.

The resulting broad reach can help published lawyers generate business, including referrals from other lawyers, by showcasing background and specialties. Bar associations and other professional organizations may invite published lawyers to speak at continuing legal education seminars and similar forums where exposure increases.

Learning and education. Writing, said former California Chief Justice Roger J. Traynor, is "thinking at its hardest."[10] Whether the forum is a newspaper or a full-length legal publication, thorough researching and careful writing can educate the writer, who may be able to apply new sources and insights in future billable client representation. The close connection among writing, thinking, and lawyering helps explain why state bar associations typically confer continuing legal education credit for some portion of time spent researching and writing or co-writing uncompensated law-related publications.

Professional satisfaction. Over the years, several of my former students in private or public law practice have told me that they pursue extracurricular writing because they feel an urge to make their voices heard outside their law offices or agencies. Their personal or professional experiences spark insights that they believe belong in the public discourse, and they seek a stimulating change of pace by engaging audiences that are considerably larger and more diverse than those typically reached in client representation.

Chapter 2 explained that in a client matter, a lawyer's immediate readership may number fewer than a dozen, and advocacy sometimes means advancing arguments and conclusions unpalatable to the lawyer. The writing's visibility might not survive resolution of the matter for which it was written. On the other hand, extracurricular writing affords lawyers greater latitude to select their own topics, fashion their own arguments and conclusions, and reach a more enduring readership that may number in the hundreds or thousands.

Daniel J. Boorstin earned a law degree and briefly practiced law before becoming one of the nation's premier social historians, a Pulitzer Prize recipient, and the Librarian of Congress.[11] The Massachusetts Bar member explained the exhilaration he felt from reaching large public audiences. Many historians "tend to write for other historians," Boorstin said, but "I want to write for the human race."[12]

Wisdom

Explanation and respect. The responsibility and rewards that may drive lawyers' extracurricular writing about law or public policy do not end the story because wisdom may weigh against the contemplated writing.

Prominent voices have long urged lawyers to do extracurricular writing that explains legal issues to lay or professional audiences, or that urges respect for law and the legal process. These writings may resemble extended public service announcements, which typically ruffle few feathers.

In 1927, for example, General John J. Pershing told the Nebraska State Bar Association that lawyers "have unusual opportunities to serve the country by helping to educate the people in their duties under our system of government."[13] A few years later, the *Missouri Bar Journal* advised that writing "newspaper articles concerning the law as it touches the lives of ordinary people . . . is an assured way to affect public relations favorably."[14]

In our own times, says Florida Chief Justice Jorge Labarga, lawyers and judges "must be willing to inform the people in plain, direct language, using the ever-increasing number of communications tools at our disposal, about the many ways we achieve justice and fulfill our role as the final guarantors of liberty under law in our system of separated powers."[15]

Throughout the nation, state bar associations urge lawyers to "speak out on public policy issues impacting the rule of law" by writing op-eds and letters-to-the-editor.[16] The aims are to nourish "an informed citizenry";[17] to "make a difference in others' lives"[18]; and to "deliver positive messages about our courts and the legal system," while "acknowledg[ing] our own problems and demonstrat[ing] what we are doing to correct them."[19] The American Bar Association invites members to write "fair and informative letters to the editor."[20]

Straining bonds. These days, however, many of lawyers' extracurricular writings about law or public policy may not merely inform readers or summon respect for law and the legal process. In our polarized times, these writings may provoke and even anger broad segments of the readership. Readers with ruffled feathers may include the writer's clients, prospective clients, and public or private employers.

Extracurricular writing about law or public policy (whether in newspapers, law reviews, bar journals, or blogs) may strain the personal bonds that sustain effective client representation. The writer may advance positions that bolster clients and causes, but a published writing whose rationale or conclusion causes strain might hurt the firm's client relations.

The lawyer's firm may have policies concerning extracurricular writing by its attorneys. Many law firm websites proudly list their lawyers' print and major blog publications, but some firms might frown on writings whose arguments and conclusions depart noticeably from ones generally held by the firm's clientele or prospective clientele, or that reflect adversely on current or prospective clients.

Government agencies and other public sector employers sometimes prohibit or discourage their lawyers from writing about subjects that the employer handles. In other public sector employment, a footnoted disclaimer sometimes makes publication permissible. ("The opinions expressed in this article are solely the author's and do not necessarily represent those of the [agency].")

Future conflicts. Lawyers' extracurricular writing may also create future conflicts that can prove personally embarrassing. When lawyers publish about law or public policy issues that touch on their practice specialty, the publication is frozen in time, available in print and electronically. Adverse consequences may follow. If the lawyer contemplates future engagements as an expert witness, for example, publication can bolster an adversary's cross-examination if the writer's conclusions and later expert testimony diverge.

Extracurricular writing's potential for future conflicts and divergence may reach even judges. In *Obergefell v. Hodges* (2015), the Supreme Court held, 5–4, that same-sex couples hold a Fourteenth Amendment due process and equal protection right to marry.[21] With voters, legislatures, or lower courts already legalizing such marriage in several states before the Supreme Court decision, dissenting Chief Justice Roberts argued that future change would have been better effected by continued evolution of the political process than by constitutional decision making.

The Chief Justice's *Obergefell* dissent quoted "a thoughtful commentator [who] observed about another issue 'The political process was moving . . . , not swiftly enough for advocates of quick, complete change, but majoritarian institutions were listening and acting. Heavy-handed judicial resolution was difficult to justify and appears to have provoked, not resolved, conflict.' "[22]

The "other issue" was abortion, and the "thoughtful commentator," writing in the *North Carolina Law Review* in 1985 about *Roe v. Wade*, was then-U.S. Circuit Judge Ruth Bader Ginsburg, who joined *Obergefell's* five-justice majority.

A ROADMAP FOR LAWYERS' JOURNALISM

Once responsibility, rewards, and wisdom point the compass toward newspaper editorial writing, the lawyer may proceed to the keyboard. *St. Louis Post-Dispatch* founder Joseph Pulitzer advanced ground rules consistent with the four fundamentals of effective writing discussed throughout this book: "Put it before them briefly so they will read it, clearly so they will appreciate it, picturesquely so they will remember it and, above all, accurately so they will be guided by its light."[23]

This ten-step roadmap proceeds from the ground rules:

1.   *Decide whether to write a letter or an op-ed.* Letters generally respond to an editorial, article, letter, or op-ed that recently appeared in the newspaper. An op-ed column may be more appropriate when the writer comments directly rather than in response.[24]

A letter may be the lawyer's sole option where the newspaper does not publish unsolicited op-eds, but only op-eds from their local staff or from nationally syndicated columnists. Even in papers that publish unsolicited op-eds, writers may stand a better chance with a letter because a half dozen or more letters typically appear for every op-ed.

Newspapers generally set the maximum length of letters at about one-third the maximum length of op-eds, about 200 words versus about 600 words. For writers who seek to make a discrete point, shorter letters may attract more readers than longer op-eds. But for topics that need more room for explanation and development, an op-ed may prove the better choice.

An op-ed may cast the writer as an expert because newspapers normally recite credentials briefly at the end of the column. But unless the letter writer's title or affiliation appears in or below the letter, the writer appears only as a reader because publication normally does not depend on expertise.

2.   *Keep pace with the swift news cycle.* If the newspaper runs only a few op-eds or letters about a hot topic, publication may favor the swift. The *New York Times* advises that op-eds and letters about hot topics "often appear within a day or two (and almost always within a week)."[25]

Some editorial pages periodically run essays about matters of general interest, but writers stand the best chance of publication with an op-ed or letter that relates to a recent, specifically identified event. The event may be one the paper has covered, or it may be one that would otherwise interest readers, including the editorial staff members who screen submissions.

3. *When possible, anticipate.* Older lawyers may recall Carly Simon's 1971 hit song, "Anticipation," which opens with "We can never know about the days to come / But we think about them anyway." If the op-ed or letter writer plans to comment on the sort of incident whose future occurrence is predictable (such as violent crime or a scheduled school bond issue), the writer may anticipate "the days to come" by writing much of the piece in advance. When the incident hits the news, the writer can have the draft and the target paper's contact information handy, and can swiftly dispatch the polished submission after adding details.

4. *Decide whether to go local, regional, or national.* Some local and regional newspapers may publish letters and unsolicited op-ed submissions only from writers within their market area,[26] but many local and regional papers also publish well-written submissions from elsewhere.[27]

If the topic is local or regional, the writer would do best by confining submissions to local or regional papers. A Boston-area school budget vote, for example, may fuel spirited debate within the local school district and perhaps nearby, but the vote would likely not stimulate interest in Los Angeles or Chicago. Where the topic concerns a national issue such as foreign relations or national tax policy, however, newspapers from coast to coast offer potential editorial forums.

5. *Choose between multiple submissions or exclusivity.* Writing op-eds or letters-to-the-editor resembles going fishing. The manuscript is the bait, and the writer seeks to catch at least one fish. But how wide should the writer cast the net?

Where the op-ed or letter concerns a topic that has received wide media coverage, the writer could submit it electronically to 25 or more newspapers nationally, hoping for publication in one or a small number. Making multiple submissions remains ethical where the writer does not promise any paper exclusivity. With a few mouse clicks, the Internet now provides contact information for a wide range of domestic and foreign newspapers. The lawyer may Google "national newspapers" or, for example, "Michigan newspapers."

The writer, however, should check a newspaper's website to see whether the paper insists on exclusive rights to op-eds or letters, at least within their market area. For smaller papers, the market area may mean a radius of a hundred miles or so. For larger newspapers, the market area may cross state lines. For some leading national newspapers (such as the *New York Times* and the *Wall Street Journal*), and for newspapers that syndicate their op-eds, the market area is nationwide.[28]

Writers grappling with exclusivity must decide whether to tempt the fate of Icarus, who flew too close to the sun with wax wings in Greek mythology and crashed into the sea. The *New York Times* and the *Wall Street Journal*, for example, promise a publication decision within ten days to two weeks.[29] Given the overwhelming volume of submissions that these papers receive, writers take a big chance. If the exclusively submitted piece is rejected, other papers may not run the now-stale commentary.

The writer's decision about exclusivity precedes submission. If the writer submits an op-ed column or letter to several newspapers and a leading paper requiring exclusivity calls to verify, it may be too late to offer to withdraw the piece from the others because the paper requiring exclusivity cannot be sure that all withdrawals will succeed.

6. *Take a position.* Editors favor op-eds and letters marked by forceful advocacy. *USA TODAY*, for example, says that unsolicited opinion pieces most likely to be accepted are marked by "timeliness (pegged to news), persuasion pitched to the other side, new information, novel arguments, revelatory insights, passion without partisanship, first-hand experience, original reporting that reveals fresh angles and makes news, expert knowledge, and/or a topic that will drive conversation on social media and in the real world."[30]

A writer might wonder whether some newspapers resist running op-eds or letters that criticize the paper's own editorial positions or general political slant, but the worry is usually misplaced. Newspapers regularly run submissions that challenge the paper's viewpoint because responsible journalists do not crave submissions that sing their praises.

The *New York Times* says that its editorial pages "need a diversity of voices and opinions about a range of topics," and that the editors remain "especially interested in finding points of view that are different from those expressed in *Times* editorials."[31] The *Hartford Courant's* op-ed submission guidelines are forthright: "We prefer viewpoints at odds with our editorial standpoint."[32]

7. *Balance civility, reason, and passion.* Most newspapers reject submitted op-eds and letters that smack of insults or defamation. Lawyers stand the best chance by combining forceful advocacy with professional dignity that would not mire the editorial pages in the mud. "It's fair to criticize the ideas and arguments of others," the *St. Louis Post-Dispatch* instructs, "but we don't allow name-calling."[33]

Op-ed and letter writers sometimes react in the heat of the moment, so they would be better off asking a spouse, friend, or colleague whether the draft balances reason and passion. If the draft seems finished late in the day, sleep on it overnight before dispatching it. (Recall Chapter 10's "4:00 Rule.") The news cycle remains swift, but anything the newspaper's editorial staff can do with the submission late in the afternoon, it can usually do first thing the next morning.

Editorial rooms move quickly, so a writer beset by second thoughts might not be able to retract a hasty submission that vents the spleen. Once an op-ed or letter is published, technology provides national and even worldwide electronic dissemination, which is usually a blessing for writers who seek to make their voices heard but can also be a curse that perpetuates later embarrassment.

8. *Cut the length.* The *Boston Globe* advises that "[t]he best way to increase the chance of having your letter chosen is to make it timely, original, and short!"[34] Even if a newspaper imposes a 600-word maximum limit on op-ed columns, a writer improves the chances for publication by weighing in at 500 words. Tight writing also helps engage the paper's readers, who may scan the editorial pages while they are on the go. Remember the cardinal rule presented in Chapter 5—the writer should finish writing before the readers finish reading.

Avoid scattershot presentations. Newspapers generally expect op-eds and letters to "[m]ake one argument thoroughly, point by point; the more detail the better."[35] "If you try to do too much," advises the *New York Times,* "you can wind up with an article that, in striving to say everything, ends up saying nothing."[36]

9. *Know the audiences.* Lawyers-as-journalists write for two audiences. The four fundamentals of good writing—conciseness, precision, simplicity, and clarity—deliver the message most effectively to both.

Unless the paper solicits the article from the lawyer, the first audience is the busy staffers who may screen dozens or hundreds of submitted op-eds and letters daily. The *Chicago Tribune* says that submissions that are "succinct rather than rambling, and that are factually accurate, stand the best chance of being selected for publication."[37] Editors may recoil from doing even minor edits because rejection is easier.

If the submission appears in print, the lawyer's second audience is the newspaper's readership in print or online. "The writing must be clear and accessible to the general reader," says the *Wall Street Journal,* because most readers are not lawyers or policy wonks conversant with jargon, manufactured acronyms, or legalese.[38] It is usually a good idea to frontload, by stating the topic and conclusion in the first paragraph, before presenting support and argument. Subject to a Rule of Reason, heed the rules of grammar, punctuation, and style.

10. *Do not overlook contemporary technologies.* Newspapers and other traditional media no longer hold a near monopoly on widespread print communication. Platforms such as Twitter, Facebook, YouTube, and LinkedIn also provide effective, swift, and sometimes more convenient, platforms for lawyers and others who wish to convey a message to sizeable audiences.

* * *

Lawyers whose writing appears on newspaper editorial pages give life to the title of broadcast journalist David Brinkley's memoir, *Everyone Is Entitled to My Opinion.*[39] "Everyone" includes the vast majority of Americans who never pass through a law school's doors.

---

[1] *Potential Strategies for Improving Public Trust and Confidence in the Courts*, 36 Ct. Rev. 63, 67–68 (Fall 1999) (quoting Seigenthaler).

[2] Trish Hall, *Op-Ed and You*, N.Y. Times, Oct. 13, 2013, https://www.nytimes.com/2013/10/14/opinion/op-ed-and-you.html (visited Aug. 14, 2020).

[3] *E.g.*, Chi. Trib., *Guide to Commentary Page*, http://www.chicagotribune.com/chi-001231 commentarypage-htmlstory.html (visited Aug. 14, 2020).

[4] David Shipley, *And Now a Word From Op-Ed*, N.Y. Times, Feb. 1, 2004, § 4, https://www.nytimes.com/2004/02/01/opinion/and-now-a-word-from-op-ed.html (visited Aug. 14, 2020).

[5] St. Louis Post-Dispatch, *How to Write a Letter to the Editor* (Apr. 20, 2010).

[6] ABA Model Rules of Prof'l Conduct, Preamble [1], [6] (2019).

[7] IV The Works of Francis Bacon 10 (1824 ed. by Baynes & Son).

[8] Arthur T. Vanderbilt, *General Education and the Law*, 4 J. Legal Educ., 255, 258 (1952) (quoting President Roosevelt).

[9] Whitney v. California, 274 U.S. 357, 377 (1927) (Brandeis, J., concurring), *overruled in part on other grounds*, Brandenburg v. Ohio, 395 U.S. 444 (1968).

[10] Roger J. Traynor, *Some Open Questions on the Work of State Appellate Courts*, 24 U. Chi. L. Rev. 211, 218 (1957).

[11] *Daniel J. Boorstin—Previous Librarians of Congress*, Library of Cong., http://www.loc.gov/about/about-the-librarian/previous-librarians-of-congress/daniel-j-boorstin/ (visited Aug. 15, 2020).

[12] Brian Lamb, *Daniel Boorstin*, in Booknotes: America's Finest Authors on Reading, Writing, and the Power of Ideas 114 (1997).

[13] John J. Pershing, *Obligations of the Bar to the State and the People*, 14 A.B.A. J. 65, 67 (Feb. 1928).

[14] *E.g., Lawyers Prepare For Group Advertising*, 3 Mo. B.J. 123, 124 (Aug. 1932).

[15] Jorge Labarga, *Justice Must Be Seen*, 90 Fla. B.J. 10 (June 2016).

[16] Mark A. Cunningham, President's Message: *Civil Discourse and the Role of the Profession In Public Policy*, 63 La. B.J. 186, 186 (Oct./Nov. 2015).

[17] Keith A. Birkes, *An Informed Citizenry . . . ,*" 1 Precedent 5 (Mo. Bar Fall 2007).

[18] Charlie J. Harris, Jr., The President's Page, *Election Year Offers a Golden Opportunity for Missouri's Lawyers*, 64 J. Mo. Bar 68, 69 (Mar.–Apr. 2008); *Image, President's Page*, 85 Mich. B.J. 16, 16 (Nov. 2006); Kelly Frels, *It's Not Just Lawyer Bashing*, 68 Tex. B.J. 194, 194 (Mar. 2005); Tod Aronovitz, President's Page, *Dignity in Law Report Card*, 77 Fla. B.J. 6, 6 (Feb. 2003).

[19] Jorge Labarga, *Justice Must Be Seen*, *supra* note 15.

[20] Roberta Cooper Ramo, *Let's Not Take It Anymore: Speaking Out Against Spurious Attacks on the Legal System Is Vital*, 82 A.B.A. J. 6 (Mar. 1996).

[21] 576 U.S. 644 (2015).

[22] *Id.* at 2625; Ruth Bader Ginsburg, *Some Thoughts on Autonomy and Equality in Relation to Roe v. Wade*, 63 N.C. L. Rev. 375, 385–86 (1985).

[23] https://www.brainyquote.com/authors/joseph-pulitzer-quotes (visited Sept. 20, 2020).

[24] *Op-Ed Guidelines for The Wall Street Journal*, Wall St. J. (Jan. 18, 2017), https://www.wsj.com/articles/oped-guidelines-for-the-wall-street-journal-1384383173 (visited Aug. 14, 2020).

[25] Thomas Feyer, *Editors' Note; The Letters Editor and the Reader: Our Compact, Updated*, N.Y. Times, May 23, 2004, https://www.nytimes.com/2004/05/23/opinion/editors-note-the-letters-editor-and-the-reader-our-compact-updated.html (visited Aug. 14, 2020).

[26] Boston Globe, *Opinion Pages Explained*, http://www.boston.com/bostonglobe/editorial_opinion/oped/oped_explained (visited Aug. 14, 2020).

[27] Ark. Democrat-Gazette, *Letters to the Editor*, http://www2.arkansasonline.com/contact/voicesform/ (visited Aug. 14, 2020) (accepts only letters from Arkansas residents); Michael Pravica,

This Is the Year to Speak Up, Christian Sci. Mon., July 1, 2004, at 19 (estimating that he had published at least 275 letters-to-the-editor in newspapers in the U.S. and around the world).

[28]   *Op-Ed Guidelines for The Wall Street Journal, supra* note 24.

[29]   *Id.*; David Shipley, *supra* note 4.

[30]   USA TODAY, *Submission Guidelines*, Sept. 29, 2016, https://www.usatoday.com/story/opinion/2016/09/29/submission-guidelines-usatoday-opinion-column-oped-howto-letters-editor/89964600/ (visited Aug. 15, 2020).

[31]   Trish Hall, *supra* note 2.

[32]   Hartford Courant, *Op-Eds Guidelines,* http://www.courant.com/hc-opeds-guidelines-story.html (visited Aug. 15, 2020).

[33]   St. Louis Post-Dispatch, *supra* note 5.

[34]   Boston Globe, *supra* note 26.

[35]   David Shipley, *supra* note 4.

[36]   *Id.*

[37]   Chi. Trib., *Guide to the Editorial Page*, http://www.chicagotribune.com/chi-001231editorialpage-htmlstory.html (visited Aug. 14, 2020).

[38]   *Op-Ed Guidelines for The Wall Street Journal, supra* note 24.

[39]   David Brinkley, Everyone Is Entitled to My Opinion (1998).

CHAPTER 16

WRITING IN LAW REVIEWS, BAR ASSOCIATION JOURNALS, AND BLOGS

▪ ▪ ▪

This chapter explores leading extracurricular writing opportunities for lawyers who wish to express themselves in prominent forums other than newspaper editorial pages. The first section concerns writing in law reviews, and the remaining two sections concern writing in state or local bar association journals, or in blogs.

LAW REVIEWS

Law reviews come from two basic sources. The first is the nation's law schools, which publish "academic law reviews." Nearly all these publications are edited by second- and third-year law students who demonstrate academic distinction, writing prowess, or both. The student editors select articles for publication, sometimes with informal advice about an article's content from the review's faculty advisor or from another faculty member who is an expert in the field. The students then collaborate with the author to edit the selected articles before publication.

A law school typically publishes both a primary law review (such as the *Columbia Law Review*), and one or more specialty law reviews (such as the *Columbia Journal of Transnational Law*). Issues of most academic law reviews are replete with law professors' articles. Articles written by judges or practicing lawyers appear, but these articles remain a minority.

The second basic source of law reviews are professional organizations that publish scholarly reviews featuring articles written by their members or other commentators. For example, the American Bar Association publishes *The Business Lawyer* and the *Antitrust Law Journal*. Similar scholarly reviews are published by other professional organizations such as the National Council of Juvenile and Family Court Judges, which publishes the *Juvenile and Family Court Journal*.

Professional organizations generally publish and edit articles that are selected after peer review (that is, after evaluation by editorial boards whose members are practicing professionals, and not upper-class law students). Law professors submit manuscripts, but other lawyers' articles relating to the organization's specialty are well represented.

Criticism

Academic law reviews suffer continuing criticism for assertedly favoring articles whose theoretical and sometimes impractical analysis is unresponsive to the roles of courts, legislatures, and other decision makers. Greater scholarly input from practicing lawyers might help bridge theory and practice.

Criticisms of academic law reviews have simmered for quite a while. In 1992, for example, U.S. Circuit Judge Harry T. Edwards chastised law professors for not "producing scholarship that judges, legislators, and practitioners can use."[1] "[M]any law schools—especially the so-called 'elite' ones," said the former University of Michigan Law School professor, "emphasiz[e] abstract theory at the expense of practical scholarship and pedagogy."[2]

In 2014, Judge Edwards signaled that little had changed in the nation's academic law reviews: "Intensely theoretical, philosophical, and empirical scholarship, which is very much in vogue in the legal academy these days, is rarely of interest or use to wide audiences. It is too abstract. Indeed, it does not even purport to address concrete issues relating to legal practice, procedure, doctrine, legislation, regulation, or enforcement."[3]

The Supreme Court has joined lower court judges. Justice Breyer, also formerly an eminent law professor, says that "law review articles have left terra firma to soar into outer space."[4] "Pick up a copy of any law review that you see," says Chief Justice Roberts, "and the first article is likely to be . . . the influence of Immanuel Kant on evidentiary approaches in 18th Century Bulgaria, or something, which I'm sure was of great interest to the academic that wrote it, but isn't of much help to the bar."[5]

"If the academy wants to deal with the legal issues at a particularly abstract, philosophical level," the Chief Justice adds, "that's great and that's their business, but they shouldn't expect that it would be of any particular help or even interest to the members of the practice of the bar or judges."[6]

This chapter is not the place to assess the contributions of academic law reviews to law reform and development. It suffices here to reiterate Chapter 2's observation that legal writers stand the best opportunity to persuade when they remain attentive to readers' circumstances.

Many law professors do pay close attention to the practical implications of their theses and argumentation, and these professors often find their well-researched law review articles cited in federal and state judicial opinions. Rigorous theoretical writing by professors and others about difficult legal and public policy issues can also provide valuable foundations for practical doctrinal development.[7] But critiques from the bench suggest that more scholarship about law and public policy written or co-written by practicing lawyers would add worthwhile perspectives that diversify and enrich the public forum. Judge Edwards advocates a balance between abstract and practical law review scholarship.[8]

Wisdom Revisited

The lawyer's decision whether to write in academic or professional-organization reviews depends on weighing the triad explored in Chapter 15—responsibility, rewards, and wisdom. For reasons similar to those presented in that chapter's discussion of lawyers' journalism, the first two considerations may favor ventures into law review writing. Now that most law schools maintain a primary law review and one or more specialty reviews that together engage a solid percentage of the student body, the favor may remain strongest among lawyers who wrote law review notes or comments during law school and who remain "bitten by the writing bug."

Wisdom, however, presents an added wrinkle not addressed in Chapter 15, the burdens imposed by time constraints. Practicing lawyers can usually write well-reasoned newspaper editorial-page submissions relatively quickly, but the same cannot be said for writing articles in academic or professional-association law reviews. Researching and writing a well-reasoned, carefully articulated law review article is tedious, time-consuming work that may intrude on a lawyer's commitments to family and clients.

Practitioners contemplating sole law review authorship should recognize that writing is a central part of the typical law professor's job description. A law professor's fixed classroom schedule—typically six hours a week at most, for about 28 weeks a year—permits time and flexibility for scholarly writing, whose production remains a professional expectation even after conferral of tenure. Even as they fulfill their commitments to class preparation, student counseling, and public service, law professors can carve out days or weeks to write with only intermittent professional interruptions.

A busy law practice is different. In today's technological age, lawyers rarely remain beyond their clients' reach during "normal business hours," as sometimes generously defined. Most weeks of the year, busy practicing lawyers work full days representing clients and their causes, so these lawyers normally would have to do the bulk of review writing largely on their own time, often in fits and starts because clients come first.

Some practicing lawyers do write law review articles alone, but other lawyers opt for co-authorship to create division of labor that better accommodates the pressures of the clock. A lawyer may collaborate with an acquaintance who is a law professor, a judge, another lawyer, an associate, or even a student law clerk in the office. Publication earns each co-author public exposure, and each typically remains responsible for the article's contents.

A practicing lawyer's co-authorship with a law professor (perhaps one of the lawyer's former professors) can create an especially productive collaboration. Each writer can bring distinct approaches and perspectives, and the article may respond to judges' critiques by combining the strengths of both theoretical and practical scholarship. Each co-author can test ideas on the other while fashioning a final product that is more likely to rest on what Justice Breyer calls "terra firma," and not venture into "outer space."

The Submissions Process

Once a lawyer decides to write or co-write a law review article, the lawyer should become familiar with the process for submitting manuscripts to academic and professional-organization reviews.[9] (Law professor co-authors will likely be familiar with the process, as would lawyers who were exposed to it as members of a primary or specialty review in law school.) These factors remain at the forefront:

1. *All academic law reviews are not created equal.* As of this writing, the United States has 203 ABA-approved law schools.[10] Virtually all law schools publish a primary law review, and most also publish one or more specialty reviews. The nation has more than 600 academic law reviews that publish about 10,000 articles each year.[11]

As might be expected, the range of academic law reviews runs the gamut from the most exclusive to the less exclusive. To survey the landscape, a good place to start is the annual *U.S. News & World Report* law school rankings.[12] These rankings have their critics, but a primary academic law review's prestige tends to follow the prestige of the law school that publishes it. Academics have also created other, sometimes controversial, rankings based on such factors as how often a particular law review's articles are cited in other law reviews.[13]

A law school's primary law review may rank higher than any of the school's specialty reviews, but many academic specialty reviews also rank high.[14] Some academic specialty reviews (for example, ones devoted to law and psychology, or to health care law) often assemble editorial boards that include students who have had career experience in the specialty before enrolling in law school. These students can influence which submissions to accept for publication, and can also enhance the post-acceptance editorial process.

Competition for publication offers can be fierce in highly ranked primary academic law reviews, which report that they sometimes receive a few thousand submissions annually but can accept only a handful (though the numbers are doubtlessly skewed because many authors submit manuscripts simultaneously to 50 reviews or more but can publish in only one). Academic specialty law reviews may receive a smaller volume of submissions because of their narrower substantive focus, so chances of publication may be enhanced for quality submissions that concern the specialty.

2. *Peer review may confer special prestige.* Among many professionals (including many law professors), publication in a leading professional organization's law review carries particular force because peer reviewers are experts rather than less experienced law students. Despite the professional-organization review's usual disclaimer that articles express only the authors' opinions and not necessarily the organization's, publication can suggest that the peer review team, and thus the organization itself, takes the article seriously.

Whether in the academic or the professional-organization world, publishing in the most prestigious forum possible remains a plus. The potential readership of a well-conceived law review writing may extend considerably beyond the immediate audience. Law review articles (like many bar journal articles, discussed below) typically reach Westlaw, Lexis, and other electronic sources, such as the law review's website or blog itself.

3. *Originality and finality matter.* Academic and professional-organization reviews ordinarily publish only manuscripts that have not appeared in other publications, wholly or in substantial part. Unless an author has an especially sterling reputation, the author stands the best chance of acceptance with a carefully proofread final manuscript that presents a fresh perspective, without bracketed material awaiting refinement, and without citations that editors must complete or conform to standard style.

The writer's submitted cover letter and accompanying abstract must make the case for publication because the "first cut" may depend on these sources alone. But even when the writer transmits a manuscript in final form with all the i's dotted and all the t's crossed, editors invariably discover matters of substance, style, or citation that invite correction. Provided that editors do not seek to interfere unreasonably with substantive matters, writers should heed Part Four of this book, which counsels restraining pride of authorship during a constructive editorial process.

Submitting the manuscript in final form helps the author maintain the upper hand during the editorial process. Academic law review writers sometimes complain, for example, about nettlesome student editors who seek to influence the substance and style of accepted manuscripts. When it turns out that an accepted manuscript remains riddled with incomplete text or inaccurate footnotes, law review standoffs are the author's own fault. When law review writers conscript student editors to do their work for them, the writers have nobody to blame but themselves when the student editors do the work.

4. *Multiple submissions and exclusivity present strategic questions.* Academic law reviews (both primary and specialty) generally permit authors to make unlimited simultaneous submissions, and most authors undoubtedly do just that. Submitting a manuscript to 50 or more academic reviews is not unusual, and may be the norm. Many peer-reviewed journals published by professional organizations require exclusive submission, plus the author's commitment to accept a publication offer without soliciting other offers.

Other things being equal, a writer stands a better chance with submissions to multiple reviews than with an exclusive submission. If one of the 50 or more submissions to academic law reviews produces a publication offer, the review usually allows the writer a week or so to consider the offer, though the writer may be able to negotiate a longer period. The writer may accept the offer immediately or within the period, or the writer may seek to "ratchet up" by requesting higher ranked academic law reviews to expedite consideration of the previously submitted manuscript before the period elapses.[15]

Publication in a peer-reviewed professional-organization journal indeed may confer prestige beyond what comes from publication in many student-edited academic law reviews. Because exclusive submission can delay the process in the event of rejection, the writer should inquire whether the professional organization, on its website or in the print edition, commits to reaching a publication decision within a reasonable period. Similar to Chapter 15's conundrum posed by exclusive submissions of newspaper op-ed columns, rejection after extended consideration may leave the article less cutting edge, and thus less appealing to other law reviews.

5. *Electronic submission of manuscripts is the norm.* Most law reviews now require or prefer manuscripts submitted electronically, and not in hard copy. The law review's website will usually state the requirements, including the permissibility or expectation of emailed submissions. For the past several years, two University of Missouri-Kansas City School of Law professors have assembled continuing updated compendia of requirements for many law reviews.[16]

Many reviews expect or require electronic submission through one of two services, Express-O or Scholastica. For a nominal fee per submission, the service transmits the manuscript, the author's cover letter, a brief abstract (which may appear atop the published article), and the author's resume (which editors may expect or require). Free of further charge, the service will transmit requests to expedite consideration of previous submissions when the author receives the first publication offer, and will transmit requests to withdraw manuscripts following the author's acceptance of an offer.

BAR ASSOCIATION JOURNALS

Most state and many local bar associations publish journals monthly, bi-monthly, or quarterly. Typically featured are researched articles written by member lawyers and selected after peer review by a bar committee. Because most bar journal authors are practicing lawyers, articles tend to combine scholarship (including recommendations for law reform where appropriate) with practical perspectives on substantive or procedural matters. The primary audience tends to be lawyers, judges, legislators, and other decision makers.

Recall from Chapter 15 the responsibility-rewards-wisdom calculus. As lawyers fulfill responsibilities to enrich discussion of the law, extracurricular writing in bar journals can deliver the short-term and long-term rewards discussed in that chapter—advertising, learning and education, and professional satisfaction. Lawyers typically cultivate face-to-face relationships one colleague at a time or in small groups, but state and local bar journals reach all lawyers who receive a copy with bar association membership. Broad reach can help published lawyers remain visible in bar association activity while they generate business, can showcase their background and expertise in a particular field of law, and can increase their knowledge about the field. Prospects of seeing their name in a byline motivate many lawyers who strive for versatility in their writing, and who hold perspectives they wish to share.

Wisdom Revisited

On the wisdom consideration, writing a bar journal article may help manage time pressures that can discourage busy practitioners from writing or co-writing law review articles. Bar journal articles tend to run about a half dozen printed pages or so, compared with the 30 pages or more that typically characterize law review articles. Bar journal articles also tend to carry a lower volume of notes than most law review articles.

Co-writing with colleagues or others remains an option. Bar journal writers can also help relieve the "time crunch" with manuscripts that concern their practice specialty and remain relevant to other lawyers. Articles sometimes adapt portions of the writer's prior briefs or other court submissions. Peer reviewers typically define relevance broadly, though most bar journals decline to publish articles that concern matters pending before a court or agency, at least without full disclosure of the pendency, and of any direct or indirect interest that the writer or a client has in the outcome.

The Submissions Process

A bar journal writer can reach the ultimate audience only by first convincing the peer reviewers, who decide whether to extend an offer to publish the manuscript. The writer's cover letter and abstract must make the case. Because a bar journal's peer reviewers and primary ultimate audience tend to be practitioners, judges, legislators, and other decision makers, supporting materials that demonstrate a practical focus usually stand the best chance. Bar journals may specify that authors themselves, and not peer reviewers or other bar association officials, are responsible for the article's accuracy, including the accuracy of quotes and citations.

Submissions guidelines usually appear in the bar journal itself or on the bar association's website. An email or telephone call to the editor or other responsible bar staff member can resolve remaining questions. To relieve prospective writers of concern that they will devote time to writing an article whose topic will be preempted, the bar journal editor may grant the writer's request to reserve a topic on an exclusive basis for a period of time. The author must generally state that the final manuscript (usually submitted electronically) has not appeared wholly or substantially in another publication. Authors also generally must acknowledge that they are making an exclusive submission, and that they commit to accept a publication offer without soliciting others.

BLOGS

In the past generation or so, swift technological advances have transformed the ways Americans go about their daily affairs. Among the most prominent innovations has been the steady rise of blogs, which are essentially online forums that feature continuous commentary about one or more designated topics. Blogs are a 21st century virtual manifestation of the face-to-face and print "marketplace of ideas" that Justice Oliver Wendell Holmes envisioned decades ago.[17]

Blogs maintained by lawyers or law professors, or ones otherwise concerning legal issues, are sometimes dubbed "blawgs." The *American Bar Association Journal* directory lists more than 4500 continually updated blawgs, a number that seems destined to continue growing.[18] The ABA reports that "law blogging appears to be flourishing."[19]

Blogs have evolved into diverse writing forums that offer web-based alternatives for disseminating information, and for sustaining discussions and online social interaction with readers. Many lawyers maintain sites of their own that seek to reach wide audiences with cutting-edge commentary. Bloggers contribute responses and commentary on interactive blogs maintained by others; when visitors sign their names rather than seek to maintain anonymity, participation in the discussion can increase professional visibility.

Some bar associations maintain blogs that provide accessible platforms for their members and other participants who are drawn to the sites. Blogs also dot the websites of an increasing number of law reviews and other print media. Many newspapers, and many radio and television stations, maintain blogs that enable readers and listeners to discuss matters raised in recent stories, or to stake out new directions.

Some lawyers also maintain or contribute to blogs devoted to topics that have little or nothing to do with law, such as cooking, childrearing, sports, or movies.[20] To increase a blog's conversational tone, and to continue attracting a following, some legal blogs intersperse discussion of such topics among their law-related postings.

Responsibility and Rewards

Blogging about law or public policy can help lawyers fulfill a professional responsibility to contribute to public discussion. These lawyers can also achieve the usual rewards of extracurricular writing—advertising, learning and education, and professional satisfaction.

One commentator says that blogging "may be the fastest growing client development tool being used by American lawyers."[21] Many law firms and lawyers maintain blogs that advertise expertise in their specialties, increase professional visibility, maintain contact with their clients, and help generate business through communication directed at other lawyers and the general public.[22]

A visible blog can attract heavy traffic, a number of readers greater than the number who will likely ever pay close attention to the blogger's writing on a client's behalf or in law reviews or bar journals. Whether a lawyer practices solo or in a firm, blogging may lead to media interviews or invitations to deliver professional presentations. Blogging can create professional relationships among regular contributors and other bloggers. Sustained presence on blogs has even reportedly led to referrals or lateral employment opportunities for some bloggers who achieve a wide audience that showcases personal reputation.[23]

Blogging can enhance a law practice by continually focusing the writer's thinking, and by disciplining the lawyer to remain current in the blog's field of law.[24] Disciplined writing remains a great way for lawyers to learn, and law reviews, bar association journals, and print media hold no monopoly on this learning in the 21st century.

Wisdom Revisited

Time constraints. Lawyers' blogging comes with pluses and minuses. On the minus side, a busy law practice may limit the time available for maintaining a visible blog's allure. The *ABA Journal* says that "[t]he commitment to blogging regularly can be intense."[25]

To stand the best chance of continually generating visitors' traffic, a blog should feature up-to-date content. Some bloggers report posting commentary more than once each day or week, and interactive blogs must be monitored for visitors' objectionable content. The ability to update continually, and to operate at the cutting edge, can create a general expectation. To attract and hold readers who might grow accustomed to the rhythm, a blogger may find it helpful to develop a formal or informal schedule for postings.

On a blog that permits interaction, writers can engage readers in ongoing give-and-take that, when thoughtfully accomplished, can stimulate participants and other viewers alike.[26] A print article is usually cast in stone once it appears; bloggers, however, can continually update postings when new developments occur, new ideas percolate, readers' responses suggest other avenues, or previously unnoticed errors or shortcomings catch the writer's eye. But the research, review, and writing that mark interaction and continual updating take time, frequently lots of time.

Some bloggers strive to meet general expectations by writing in teams of two or more who create a workable division of labor,[27] but each member remains responsible for entries that bear the member's name, and for the blog itself. The team approach resembles co-authorship and, similar to the law review and bar journal arrangements discussed above, can help balance the rewards of successful blogging, the demands of a busy law practice, and the press of other personal and professional commitments.

Potential impermanence. Another "minus" of blogging is that unlike traditional print publications whose entries are permanent once published, blog sites may be abandoned or terminated without notice or expectation. In 2013, the *New York Times* reported on a study which found that "49 percent of the hyperlinks in Supreme Court decisions no longer work."[28] The *Times* characterized the disappearing cites as "web links to nowhere," and concluded that "[t]he modern Supreme Court decision is increasingly built on sand."[29] To be on the safe side, bloggers who wish to preserve their written contributions for possible future use should maintain personal copies.

Convenience and flexibility. Heading blogging's "plus" side are convenience and flexibility. More swiftly than newspaper op-eds or letters-to-the-editor, blogs enable lawyers to write short commentaries about the law (and even about subjects having little or nothing to do with the law) for legally trained and lay audiences alike. Longer commentaries and full-length essays may also appear.

Law review articles can run 30 researched pages or more, and may feature dense footnotes. Bar journal articles also require sustained research and writing. Bloggers may write extended essays or attach lengthy articles or other documents or links, but thoughtful, provocative blog postings frequently consist of a few sentences or paragraphs.[30]

Blog postings appear quickly, without the weeks or months of editing and other intermediation that can slow law review articles and other print publications, and that can leave some print publications obsolete before they appear.

Blog postings can resemble print journalism in length and content, but bloggers do not have to continually watch word count and worry that a newspaper will reject the submission for being a sentence or two over the formal or informal limit. The absence of incessant word counting can spur a blogger's creativity and self-expression, though careful bloggers heed the standard presented in Chapter 5—the writer should finish writing before readers finish reading. When managing a writing's length in hard copy or in electronic format, central bywords (discussed in Chapter 5) remain self-discipline and measured brevity.

Regardless of length, successful law blogging depends on maintaining quality. Some bloggers report that they can sometimes generate postings in a few minutes or an hour or so, but the most effective blog entries are not simply slapdash efforts designed to fill space. Serious visitors want carefully conceived thoughts that are reviewed, carefully expressed, and well-grounded in doctrine or reasonable argument drawn from doctrine.

Typographical errors, misspellings, and similar flaws can raise readers' doubts about substantive accuracy that arise whenever legal writing noticeably fails to measure up. Timeless advice from 18th century British poet, essayist, and biographer Samuel Johnson defines the essence of lawyers' personal responsibility in 21st century blogs: "What is written without effort is in general read without pleasure."[31]

THE BOUNDARIES OF EXTRACURRICULAR WRITING

A lawyer might be satisfied with publishing in one extracurricular forum. Provided that the lawyer secures the necessary copyright permissions and discloses prior publication, however, publishing in one forum need not signal the end.

For example, the lawyer might publish a newspaper op-ed column and then expand all or part of it into a law review or bar journal article, or even a book. Or the lawyer might begin with a law review or bar journal article before spinning off one or more op-ed columns or blog postings.

One way or another, the lawyer's extracurricular writing demands graceful expression because it remains unofficial commentary that ordinarily no one *must* read. As Chapter 2 discussed, it pays to Know the Audience and to Earn the Right to a Reader.

---

1   Harry T. Edwards, *The Growing Disjunction Between Legal Education and the Legal Profession*, 91 Mich. L. Rev. 34, 34 (1992).

²   *Id.; see also, e.g.,* Harry T. Edwards, *The Role of Legal Education in Shaping the Profession,* 38 J. Legal Educ. 285, 291 (1988) ("Law professors seem more and more often content to talk only to each other—or perhaps to a few colleagues in other academic disciplines—rather than deal with the problems facing the profession.").

³   Harry T. Edwards, *Another Look at Professor Rodell's* Goodbye to Law Reviews, 100 Va. L. Rev. 1483, 1484 (2014). *See also, e.g.,* Richard A. Posner, Divergent Paths xii, 33 (2016) (identifying a "chasm between the academy and the judiciary"); Sandra L. Lynch, *Interview Conducted by Bryan A. Garner,* 15 Scribes J. Legal Writing 61, 73 (2013). (quoting U.S. Circuit Judge Sandra L. Lynch: "[T]here are so few law-review articles that are really of use to judges.").

⁴   Stephen G. Breyer, *Response of Justice Stephen G. Breyer,* 64 N.Y.U. Ann. Surv. Am. L. 33, 33 (2008) (citation omitted).

⁵   Jonathan H. Adler, *Chief Justice Roberts Reads Law Reviews, After All,* Wash. Post, Mar. 21, 2015).

⁶   *Id.*

⁷   *E.g.,* Cass Sunstein, *In Praise of Jargon,* Chron. Higher Educ., Feb. 14, 2016.

⁸   Harry T. Edwards, *supra* note 3 at 1484.

⁹   For constructive discussions of the law review submission process, see, e.g., Eugene Volokh, Academic Legal Writing ch. 23 (4th ed. 2010) (discussion geared to law student writers, but with information instructive to lawyers); Gerald Lebovits, *Academic Legal Writing: How to Write and Publish,* 78 N.Y. St. B.J. 64 (Jan. 2006) (discussion geared to lawyers).

¹⁰   Am. Bar Ass'n, *ABA-Approved Law Schools,* http://www.americanbar.org/groups/legal_education/resources/aba_approved_law_schools.html (visited Aug. 10, 2020).

¹¹   *E.g.,* David Segal, *What They Don't Teach Law Students: Lawyering,* N.Y. Times, Nov. 20, 2011, at A22.

¹²   U.S. News & World Rep., *2021 Best Law Schools,* https://www.usnews.com/best-graduate-schools/top-law-schools/law-rankings (ranked in 2020) (visited Aug. 14, 2020).

¹³   *See, e.g.,* John Doyle, *The Law Reviews: Do Their Paths of Glory Lead But to the Grave?,* 10 J. App. Prac. & Process 179, 181–85 (2009).

¹⁴   Wash & Lee Sch. of Law, Law Lib., *Law Journals: Submissions and Ranking,* 2007–2014 (2015).

¹⁵   Eugene Volokh, *supra* note 9 at 267–68.

¹⁶   Allen Rostron & Nancy Levit, *Information for Submitting Articles to Law Reviews & Journals* (last revised July 2020).

¹⁷   Abrams v. United States, 250 U.S. 616, 630 (1919) (Holmes, J., dissenting) ("[T]he best test of truth is the power of the thought to get itself accepted in the competition of the market.").

¹⁸   Am. Bar Ass'n, *ABA Journal Blawg Directory,* https://www.abajournal.com/blawgs (visited Aug. 10, 2020).

¹⁹   Molly McDonough, Am. Bar Ass'n, *The 2015 ABA Journal Blawg 100: The State of the Legal Blogosphere,* 101 A.B.A. J. 54, 55 (Dec. 2015).

²⁰   *E.g.,* Sarah Kellogg, *Do You Blog?,* 17 S.C. Law. 30, 38 (July 2005).

²¹   Kevin O'Keefe, *Law Blogs: The Great Equalizer,* 4 Precedent 22, 22 (MoBar No. 2 Spring 2010).

²²   Molly McDonough, *supra* note 20 at 55.

²³   *E.g.,* Margaret M. DiBianca, *Delaware Lawyers Who Blog,* 27 Del. Law. 24, 25 (Winter 2009/2010).

²⁴   *Id.*

²⁵   Molly McDonough, *supra* note 20 at 56.

²⁶   *E.g.,* Ruth Carter, *Social Media For Lawyers: Top 10 Blogging Tips For Attorneys,* 48 Ariz. Atty. 24, 25 (Apr. 2012).

²⁷   *E.g.,* Margaret M. DiBianca, *supra* note 23 at 25.

²⁸   Adam Liptak, *In Supreme Court Decisions, Web Links to Nowhere,* N.Y. Times, Sept. 14, 2013, at A13 (reporting on study by Jonathan Zittrain and Kendra Albert).

²⁹   *Id.*

³⁰   *E.g.,* Dan X. Nguyen, *Marketing Your Practice,* 52 Orange Cty. Law. 30, 30 (July 2010).

³¹   Paul Bowden, Telling It Like It Is 259 (2011) (quoting Johnson).

POSTSCRIPT

HOW WRITING CAN SHARPEN PERSONAL DECISION MAKING

■ ■ ■

The 2004 National Football League Draft was fast approaching, and the last-place San Diego Chargers held the first selection overall. Their expected choice, University of Mississippi quarterback Eli Manning, was no stranger to the NFL's affairs because his father, former New Orleans Saints quarterback Archie Manning, and his older brother, Indianapolis Colts quarterback Peyton Manning, had preceded him to stardom.

Eli told the Chargers that he would not sign if the team selected him, and he intimated that he would instead re-enter the 2005 draft, expecting selection by another team. Sitting out the 2004–2005 season would mean losing a year's multimillion-dollar income in his athletic prime, but media reports indicated that the young quarterback believed he could get a more favorable long-term contract from a team in a major media market.

San Diego did pick Eli first. But to avoid a stalemate that would have left the team with nothing to show for its envied first-round position, the Chargers immediately traded him to the New York Giants. The rest is history. Just ask any Giants fan about the team's Super Bowl victories in 2008 and 2012.

"WRITING IS REFINED THINKING"[1]

How did future two-time Super Bowl Most Valuable Player Eli Manning reach his high-stakes decision to spurn the San Diego Chargers and contemplate a season on the sidelines? "Eli did what I have always suggested in making big decisions," said his father. "I'm a legal pad guy. He took out a legal pad, drew a line down the middle, and put the pluses on one side and the minuses on the other side. It wasn't even close, so he went with it."[2]

At least three recent Presidents—Richard Nixon, Jimmy Carter, and George H.W. Bush—were also "legal pad guys" who often marshalled their thoughts by listing pros and cons in two columns as they wrestled with major decision making.[3] Other leaders reportedly reliant on such written lists include Senator and Secretary of State Hillary Rodham Clinton; Senators Mitt Romney, Lloyd Bentsen, and Sam Nunn; Health and Human Services Department Secretary Sylvia Mathews Burwell; Treasury

Secretary Robert Rubin; and governors Michael Dukakis and Pete Wilson.[4] This technique of decision making aided by listing pros and cons in writing holds a long pedigree; in 1952, for example, Ohio Senator Robert A. Taft composed a list to help him decide whether to challenge General Dwight D. Eisenhower for the Republican presidential nomination.[5]

These leaders recognized that committing arguments to paper can often focus decision making more clearly than oral contemplation. Prominent judges share this recognition. "All of us have had seemingly brilliant ideas that turned out to be much less so when we attempted to put them to paper," explained U.S. Circuit Judge Wade H. McCree, Jr.[6] "Every conscientious judge has struggled, and finally changed his mind, when confronted with the 'opinion that won't write.' "[7]

"The act of writing," summarized U.S. Circuit Judge Frank M. Coffin, "tells what was wrong with the act of thinking."[8]

CHOOSING THE FORMAT

Chapter 2's image of the Legal Writer's Theater casts the writer as the performer and readers as the audience. But the writer listing pros and cons is both performer and audience.

Rather than listing pros and cons in two columns to expose tentative decisions that "won't write," lawyers or others might draft longer passages, or even short informal essays. Personal preference determines the most effective format because the point-counterpoint is normally for the writer's eyes only, unless the writer shares the document with others.

Regardless of the format, writing can influence not only lawyers' personal and professional decision making, but also advice that lawyers provide clients about how to reach their own decisions on important matters within or outside the scope of representation. Some clients may already understand how committing arguments to writing can stimulate disciplined reflection, but other clients may not.

Written decision making should come naturally to lawyers because it remains central to the American judicial system, and thus to the way law schools prepare students for brief writing and other practical professional skills. In a bench trial or an action tried to an advisory jury, Rule 52(a)(1) of the Federal Rules of Civil Procedure requires the court to "find the facts specially and state its conclusions of law separately." Appellate courts commonly hand down decisions with signed opinions (including majority, plurality, concurring, and dissenting opinions), *per curiam* opinions, or unpublished opinions that articulate reasons.

RULE 52(a)(1)

The trial court's written findings of fact and conclusions of law focus appellate review, enable application of preclusion doctrines, and seek to inspire confidence in the trial court's decision making.[9] But federal courts of appeals recognize the paramount purpose of Rule 52(a), "that of evoking care on the part of the trial judge in ascertaining the facts."[10] The Supreme Court recognizes that "laymen, like judges, will give more careful consideration to the problem if they are required to state not only the end result of their inquiry, but the process by which they reached it."[11]

In *United States v. Forness* in 1942, the U.S. Court of Appeals for the Second Circuit thoughtfully explained Rule 52(a)'s paramount purpose.[12] The unanimous panel included Judge Charles E. Clark, the chief drafter of the Federal Rules of Civil Procedure and an authority on their meaning and application.

Writing for the *Forness* panel, Judge Jerome Frank said this: "[A]s every judge knows, to set down in precise words the facts as he finds them is the best way to avoid carelessness. . . . Often a strong impression that, on the basis of the evidence, the facts are thus-and-so gives way when it comes to expressing that impression on paper."[13] Judges hold no monopoly on this knowledge of writing's influence.

APPELLATE DECISION MAKING

An appellate court's full opinion or more abbreviated writing demonstrates that the court considered the parties' arguments, facilitates further review on remand or by a higher court, and helps determine the decision's meaning as precedent. But the writing's capacity to sharpen the decision makers' internal thought processes looms large, as do district court writings under Rule 52(a).

Chief Justice Charles Evans Hughes found "no better precaution against judicial mistakes than setting out accurately and adequately the material facts as well as the points to be decided."[14] "The process of writing signed opinions," explained Justice Ruth Bader Ginsburg, is "a testing venture."[15] "I don't really understand any case until I write it," says Justice Elena Kagan.[16]

THE "HUMAN FACTOR"

Written personal or professional decision making sometimes has its limitations. When emotions and other intangibles weigh in, the outcome does not necessarily depend on which side of the legal pad's ledger—pro or con—recites the longer list. Writing in *Forness*, Judge Frank acknowledged that "fact-finding is a human undertaking" that "can, of course, never be perfect and infallible."[17]

Naturalist Charles Darwin, for example, listed the pros and cons of getting married before he proposed to his future wife.[18] His list contained 13 "cons" and only nine "pros," but he married her anyway.[19] The couple remained married for 43 years and had 10 children.

When Thomas P. Schneider's term as U.S. Attorney for the Eastern District of Wisconsin ended a few years ago, he weighed offers to join large influential law firms at handsome salaries, plus friends' suggestions that he cap his 29-year career as a prosecutor by running for state attorney general. The *Milwaukee Journal Sentinel* reported that Schneider took a legal pad and divided the page into two columns lengthwise, one for pros and the other for cons.[20]

Then his wife stepped in and told him to cast the pad aside. "This is not a legal brief," she told him, "This is your life."[21]

The rest is history, as it was with Giants quarterback Eli Manning. Schneider rejected politics and lucrative private law practice to become executive director of COA Youth and Family Centers, an agency dedicated to improving poor Milwaukee neighborhoods by enhancing opportunities for needy children and their families. The human factor, an emotional inner sense, tilted the scale and ultimately carried the day for the career prosecutor.

"I've always loved working with kids," Schneider told the *Journal Sentinel*, "What I really care about is how do you make a positive difference in this world."[22] This personal calibration of reason and passion cannot be committed to dual columns on a legal pad.

---

[1]   Stephen King, On Writing: A Memoir of the Craft 131 (2000).

[2]   Rick Cleveland, *Mannings Endure Boos, Slurs and Media Criticism . . . and Life Goes On*, Clarion-Ledger (Jackson, Miss.), May 2, 2004, at 1D.

[3]   Robert W. Merry, Taking on the World: Joseph and Stewart Alsop 548 (2012) (Pres. Nixon); Michael D. Langan, *Nixon in 3-D: How He Looks In the 21st Century*, Buffalo (N.Y.) News, July 5, 2015, at C30 (Pres. Nixon); Mindy Fetterman, *CEO's Advise the President*, USA TODAY, June 28, 1991, at 1B (Pres. Carter); Susan Fraker et al., *B-1 No, Cruise Yes*, Newsweek, July 11, 1977, at 15 (Pres. Carter); Anne Reilly Dowd, *How Bush Manages the Presidency*, Fortune, Aug. 27, 1990, at 68 (Pres. Bush).

[4]   Neela Banerjee, *Clinton Pushes Back Against Critics on Benghazi*, L.A. Times (June 15, 2014) (Sec'y Clinton); Alessandra Stanley, *At Times, Nice Guys Finish Second*, N.Y. Times, Jan. 24, 2014, at C1 (Gov. Romney); Donald M. Rothberg, *With a War On, Even Democrats Want Bush For President*, Lewiston (Idaho) Morning Trib., Feb. 17, 1991, at 1A (Sen. Bentsen); Eric Schmitt, *Even G.O.P. Asking Nunn Not To Retire From Senate*, N.Y. Times, Oct. 2, 1995, at A10 (Sen. Nunn); Linda Feldmann, *Who Is Sylvia Mathews Burwell? The Likely New Face of Obamacare*, Christian Sci. Mon., Apr. 11, 2014 (Sec'y Burwell); Sharon Walsh, *Rubin Will Share Helm at Citigroup*, Wash. Post, Oct. 27, 1999, at E1 (Sec'y Rubin); Stuart K. Spencer, *Dukakis Picking His Second Place*, L.A. Times, July 3, 1988, at pt. 5, p. 3 (Gov. Dukakis); Jerry Roberts, *Wannabe Wilson Searches His Soul*, San Francisco Chronicle, Mar. 5, 1995, at 7 (Gov. Wilson).

5   David Halberstam, The Fifties 205 (1993).

6   Wade H. McCree, Jr., *Bureaucratic Justice: An Early Warning*, 129 U. Pa. L. Rev. 777, 790–91 (1981); *see also, e.g.*, Robert E. Keeton, Judging 137 (1990) ("the necessity of explaining disciplines choice"); Ruth Bader Ginsburg, *Workways of the Supreme Court*, 25 Thos. Jefferson L. Rev. 517, 526 (2003) ("At least once each of the nine terms I have served on the Court, an opinion writer finds that the conference position, in whole or in part, 'won't write,' so the writer ends up taking a different view.").

7   Wade H. McCree, Jr., *supra* note 6 at 790–91.

8   Frank M. Coffin, The Ways of a Judge 57 (1980).

9   9C Charles Alan Wright & Arthur R. Miller, Federal Practice and Procedure § 2571, at 219–22 (3d ed. 2008).

10   United States v. Forness, 125 F.2d 928, 942 (2d Cir. 1942).

11   United States v. Merz, 376 U.S. 192, 199 (1964).

12   Forness, *supra* note 10, 125 F.2d 928 (2d Cir. 1942).

13   *Id.* at 942.

14   Charles Evans Hughes, The Supreme Court of the United States 64 (1928).

15   Ruth Bader Ginsburg, *Remarks on Writing Separately*, 65 Wash. L. Rev. 133, 139 (1990).

16   Justice Elena Kagan, *Interview With Bryan A. Garner*, www.lawprose.org (video, part 3) (July 15, 2015).

17   Forness, *supra* note 10, 125 F.2d at 943.

18   Malcolm Jones, *Who Was More Important: Lincoln or Darwin?*, Newsweek, July 14, 2008, at 30; Mary Harris Russell, *2 Views of a Remarkable Scientist*, Chi. Trib., Jan. 3, 2009, at 3.

19   William Hartston, *Ten Things You Never Knew About . . . Charles Darwin*, The Express (England), Jan. 7, 2009, at 30.

20   Gina Barton, *From Courthouse to Social Service Agency*, Milwaukee J. Sentinel, Nov. 17, 2002, at 1B.

21   *Id.*

22   *Id.*

INDEX

References are to Pages